HOW TO TRAIN A WILD PUPPY DOG NAMED MANLEY

HOW TO TRAIN A WILD PUPPY DOG NAMED MANLEY

A NOVEL: NEW EDITION. BASED ON SOME REAL-LIFE EVENTS

E Lloyd Kelly

E Lloyd Kelly

Introduction

When East meets West. After having heard it said once too many times that, all men are dogs. I thought to myself: if that's true! Who then is the dog trainer who trained these pups and taught them those cunning, clever doggy tricks? And a book was born, the "Manley book". How to Train a Wild Puppy Dog Named Manley is a Jamaican-yardy, hardcore romance novel, packed full of wry humor, metaphoric terms, ambiguity, and innuendos, for your reading pleasure.

Libby Dahoust is a spectacularly beautiful girl of East Indian origin and a medical student at McGill University. And Manley? Manley Jaxtan Woodhardt is an overexposed, oversexed Jamaican-born divorcee on the rebound. Their background dictates that they should take diametrically opposite paths to life in general, and to love in particular. However, when both their paths were to have crossed, while on route to higher learning. Sparks began to fly. Hearts got tangled up in the mix and a rocky road seemed the only way forward. Will they manage to make it out, in one piece? Only time will tell. Not all men are dogs, no. Some are jack-as-is and monkeys too.

Note: The names and characters depicted in this book are fictitious and not to be construed as being real, nor associated with any actual person living or dead. Mature subject matters are included, and parental guidance is strongly advised. So. Let's talk about sex-baby, and dogs?

This is copyright-protected work. © 2020 By E. Lloyd Kelly. All rights reserved.

Chapter One: Catch a Sneaky, Peaky Puppy in Action

I think I'm beginning to like my mother's side of the family just a little too much now, for my own good. Yes. My physician was right, the good doctor had diagnosed that I had a severe case of swelling skin syndrome. And then, he prescribed for me, or at least he'd suggested some random remedies. Which was to have included me jumping off of it, or into the deep end of something. What it was I can't quite remember. I think it was into the deep end of some ice-cold water. Or something like that. I particularly liked the "deep" part of the whole thing though, if nothing else.

...

Monday, August 6th, 2012. Downtown Montreal Quebec. Still have twenty minutes to go before I'm done with this job and move on to the next. She needs to get her welding done. And? I've been putting off the oil change thing for way too long too. Even a rickety old car needs its regular oil change. Right?

So there I was, still reeling from the loss of my marriage to Aylene. And flogging myself black and blue for having gone so badly off-track in that arena. Life had suddenly begun to shine a light of hope in my direction again. My business was taking off. And I was, like, doing okay at the self-improvement thing one might say. But old habits tend to die hard, so there I was. Back down the road which leads right back to the lifestyle of my teenage past. Back to my old ways, back to my old puppy dog ways. Messing around with a girl I didn't know that well. Didn't really like. And sure as hell, didn't want. But she did have something that I really wanted back then, and badly so.

On the way there, I stopped at the Caribbean Kitchen restaurant to grab myself a bite to eat. I have to get her something special too. I knew she liked Roti, so I picked up two. One for her, the other for me. I also grabbed two drinks, a soft one and a hard one. The soft one was for her, the hard one for me. One can't have Roti without something cool and refreshing to go down with it. Can he? Like, something to wash it down. I needed something long and strong. Actually, she needed the "something long." That's why I was going there. I needed the strong one, the drink that is. It was a rather hard day at work that particular day but whenever she calls, I run to her. She said she was bored. Which is always a code word for me to get there and get there fast.

"I've got the excitement that you need." I'd said in response, "And I'm coming to you, babe. With wings on my feet."

She was at work at the time, if one could call that sort of thing work. She was babysitting the kid. Right at that moment when she'd called me. She was damn nearly asleep too, lying there on the couch. The baby was sleeping alright, and she? She was lying there along-side the baby half asleep herself. Some kind of "work." She did wake up well enough to open up the door and let me in when I got there. She was mighty happy to have the Roti and drink too. All of the red-eyed sleepy-look quickly dissipated into a wide wake and alerted Miss Mira. Name-calling me: sweetheart, darling baby. "My" sweetheart, my darling baby.

Even if it's only in her delusional, demented way of thinking. If while in the process of doing all that, it leads to getting me what I want? I can be anything.

Meanwhile, I was quick in getting in and out of the shower. I had to go and freshen up after the hard day at work before moving on to the next stage.

She was slightly hunched over the washbasin in the bathroom as I stepped out of the shower. She was brushing her teeth. I walked up behind her and kissed her neck. Her plaited dirty brown hair was tied up in a ponytail there. Of course, it was her hair. She bought it so it was hers. No?

My ready and willing hand reached down and around her waist. Sliding smoothly over her silky-smooth chocolate brown skin and then back up to cup the plumb, warm begging mammary bulbs. Caressing them with even, purposeful strokes. Man, what a luscious load. What! If I love them? Course I do.

My thumb and forefinger meanwhile were concentrating on the nippled spouts. The bathrobe was very cooperative too. Would have slid off her shoulder and tumbled to the floor at her feet. As she turned around and cupped my face in her hands, she kissed me. I went to work on those lips before she, Ms. Mira, pushed my head down where the hand was busily working moments before. Now the right hand is gripping hard at the cheeks, the other cheeks. While pulling her up and in towards the real hard facts of the matter. Ugh, hmm, she grunted, as she pulled slightly away.

"Let's go into my room," she said...

"Your room? Sure. This may be the place where you crash and hang out whenever you're on the job. But this is not your room. This is the house and home of your mistress. Your employer, your boss. So neither of us should be in this room, or any other room here in this house, not you, not me for that matter. None of us. Until that day when we bought and owned the damn crib." Of course, I didn't say any of that to her. Not then, not ever. This was just a little best-buddy exchange between Bubbles and me. There was too much urgency in the task at hand for me to be thinking of anything beyond the obvious.

"Come on," I said, "let's not spoil this babe." The bathrobe on the bathroom floor will suffice."

She took hold of one of the many strong limbs hanging off this hunk of a strong tree. And drag me into the bedroom. Both of us butt-naked and heated up to a fever pitch, this waggy-tailed puppy dog willingly followed. Heck, you're the boss here, I mused within. You'll always be, in said sorts of situations.

The baby cried and gyrated her hands and feet. As she rolled over and sat up. All of that moaning, groaning, bumping and grinding must have woken her up prematurely. Now she's the one who needs all of the attention. She most certainly needed it more than me at this point. And sweet and kind Miss Mira is not one who is known to be withholding much-needed pleasure from anyone. Not from me, and certainly not from a crying baby. She picked the baby up and brought her right there in the bed with us. After filling out the tiny hands with the coveted prize, the bottle of warmed-up mother's breast milk. The kid seemed much more interested in figuring me out though. Much more so than she was to be on the task of nourishing herself with a bottled meal hanging by tiny teeth from her mouth. As she bounced and tumbled around. She just kept on twisting and turning around to stare at the stranger lying right there in the bed. The very same bed that she usually crawls all over. Without ever seeing such a face as this sneaky little puppy dog's anywhere around, until now. "Huh-huh," I grunted from within, I think that if I hang around this joint much longer, this kid might one day grow up calling me Papa. Hell no, I said, I'm out of here.

...

Unbeknownst to either of us, we were being watched. Yep, our every move was being monitored and recorded by a private eye. Or maybe it was a set of private eyes? Not sure but. As was to be revealed later on. We were captured and locked down in a pan. Oh, the wonders of technology. Mira called again on the following day, "We're in trouble," she said, "big trouble."

"I want you to come upstairs right this minute Mira," Miss Kentise, (that's what Mira calls her), Mrs. Kentise had said that she wanted her upstairs right away.

Mrs. Addasa Kentise, her mistress, wanted to talk to her, and it couldn't wait. So, she picked up the baby and hopped up on the stairs. There was no subtlety to the reveal. The screenshot was the first thing that hit her eyeballs as soon as she entered the living room. A picture-perfect portrait of the man standing there in the basement sitting room, right beside the baby sleeping in the crib. There was no doubt as to who the person in the picture was. And furthermore, there was no doubt as to what the purpose of the meeting with her mistress was about either. Mira swallowed hard, "I'm in deep doo-doo," she said to herself.

"Just a couple of quick questions for you Miss Mira. And just as quickly I'd like to get the truth from you. Who's this person in my house? Standing over my sleeping baby? And why is this person here, in my house?" She punctuated each word. Words would not come when she tried to respond.

"I, I, I don't know, I don't know wo-wo what to say." She stuttered.

"You don't know this person who's with you in my house?"

"Yes," she replied.

"Yes-what?"

"Yes, I know who he is..."

"Then tell me, who is he? Tell me."

"He's my friend, a-a, a friend of mine. His name is ma-ma, Manley."

"Why was he in my house? What was he doing here?"

"I was alone and bored, and when Sarah went to sleep, I-I just needed someone to talk to and..."

"So you invited him here?"

"Yes - ma'am."

"That'll be all for now - Mira. I'll have a lot of thinking to do before I decide on my next move. Now, get out of my face." Mira turned around and headed briskly back down the steps towards the basement apartment. She was shaking like a leaf against the rushing wind and wiping the tears from her eyes with the back of her hand. What does this mean for her? Is this going to be the end of the job? She was wondering. She never knew how much, nor was she even sure if she liked or disliked the job before this. But suddenly, she felt very scared. She didn't want to lose this job, at least not yet.

"One more thing Mira." Mrs. Kentise called out to her just before she closed the door at the bottom of the staircase behind her. On the way back to the basement apartment. "I need the contact information for this person, your friend. I'm going to have to talk to him too."

"Okay ma'am," said Mira, closing the door.

Chapter Two: Love to Die For

Even though she knew that she couldn't love me, she still did want me, and I was going stone-cold out of my cotton-picking mind for wanting her too. Libby was 24. As for me, I was 34 years of age at the time. The forces on either side of this socio-divide were unrelenting. Was this a love to die for? Maybe, but then again, maybe not.

Libby Dahoust is her name, I'm Manley, Manley Jaxtan Woodhardt. I met her there in the study hall. Well, I saw her there for the very first time on the orientation evening. We were both volunteering our services there, but really, we only did meet and greet in a strange kind of way at the food counter in the pizzeria across the street at Sherbrooke Street and McGill College. She's a straight-A medical student of Indian descent. Straight shiny black hair and chocolate brown skin. And me? I'm just barely skimming my way through a course in computer programming and design. A West Indian-born dark-skinned dreadlock wanna-be at the time. My dreads were just beginning to take shape but I sure have got the physique and the good looks to work it well. Well, so they used to say in those days. I'm the quintessential West Indian man. That's what they also said. I had no reason to doubt them.

She's very shy and reserved. Or so it would have seemed at first sight to many. Including me. Her head is always in books or papers. Until I caught her eyeing me there that day. Or should I say, we were eyeing each other? I was looking at her over the pizza and coke in front of me on the table. She must have felt the burning, piercing gaze because. She looked up from the paper and flashed a quick glance and a smile my way. Then revert back to the paper before her there, on the table.

The crushed-up paper plate and empty drink container that was also there on the table in front of her. Suggested to me that she had already finished her meal and was using the rest of the time there studying. Whether it was to be the papers or something else, she was, yes, studying. Every now and then she would sneak other peaks my way, until. She was either done with her studies or she had had her fill with somebody. She picked up her belongings and shook her wide-open palm in a jolly and gay little wave at me on the way out, "Bye!" She whispered. That's how it was to have gotten started. Think I may have ruined her studies for a brief moment there though. The only thing she seemed to be wanting to study there for a while after I walked in, was me. But...

...

What a difference a day can make sometimes. From mesmerizing eye deals on day one. To just "hi," and not even so much as a goodbye the next day. On day two, she hurriedly finished off what was left of the meal she was having, and was gone before my order even came up. I watched her as she crossed the street. Mount up onto the sidewalk and continue on through the oval-shaped entry gate that leads into the park and onto the campus grounds. She never even turned to look back. She must have had some sense talked into her last night I thought to myself. Or maybe something even more sinister than that.

"One doesn't have time to look around or mess around just before sitting and passing an exam." She told me later on after she had learned how to confide in me. I had asked her about the detached persona and the swift escape that afternoon. She said she had to go sit an exam and wasn't in the mood for a distraction.

"Wow, is that what I am? A distraction?"

...

Her father was a physician in his Asiatic homeland but had to settle to drive a taxi cab here in his new country of residence. The family also owns and operates a grocery store in the Cote des Neige area: D&D Tropical Products. The elder Dahoust woman - Luba Dahoust and Kamal the son is the face of that business. Whenever Kamal is not chauffeuring his sister - Libby. He can be found either in the store there or he would be driving the delivery truck, a cube-shaped white Isuzu truck.

They were nine and ten. Her brother and her when he (the father), threatened to kill him (the brother) because. He caught him trying to make out with his sister (Libby) on the basement sofa. He nearly killed the poor boy with licks. And then warned him that: "If I ever get wind of you even so much as to get close to her again, I swear to God (or Allah,) I will kill you." Then the second round of licks came and did not stop until Kamal lay sprawled out on the floor, seemingly lifeless. Panicking, Luba, their mother. Sprang into action and picked him up. She then went to work nursing him: back to life, back to health, and now? Back to the current reality of the "Libby story," not me. Libby, all the while, while that (the murdering of his brother by his own dear father) was happening. She was slumped in a corner in a fetal position, barely daring even so much as to breathe.

...

"We were just experimenting," she told me. "We were nine and ten. He was ten, I was nine. And no," she'd said when I asked her further. "Dad didn't punish me for it, at least not in terms of the flagging. He laid all of the blame on Kamal. Still isn't quite sure why but... For the next four to five years we were hardly ever seen in the same room together. Or in any close proximity to each other, alone." I then took the risk and probed even further. I inquired if she thought that she had any role to play in what had happened.

"At the time not so much," she said. But as the years went by, I became somewhat more and more self-conscious and started to wonder if I might have led him on.

"I was old enough to have known better," she acknowledged. She did admit to me that it felt really good though and that she must have wanted it. She could have stopped it, she said, but she didn't. "Did you do it?" I further asked, "I mean. How far did you manage to get into it?"

"Why am I sitting here pouring out my soul to you though?" She blurted out, "I don't even know you, and..." that was when. She pushed back the chair and got up. Took up her bag and paper folder and walked out. Without even looking back. That was the end of that conversation, for the time being at least.

Her brother and she seem to be very tight nowadays though. For want of a better term. He's the one who dropped her off and picked her up from school almost every day. One of the rare exceptions to that routine was to become my greatest ally.

Chapter Three: Seeing Things in Black, and White

It would eventually become necessary for me to come up with a plan to blackmail Mrs. Kentise into surrendering. In the same manner, as she had done it to me. That was after I had gotten hooked on Libby. Some of her very own tools of the trade would come in very handy in bringing that about too, tools such as the camera and the sound recorder. Voice recording apps too, on the phone. It was long after it had become clear to me that: the only thing she was going to be doing with the evidence she had gathered on me being in her house screwing around with her helper was to use it to try and blackmail me into doing the exact same sort of thing for her, and to her. After deciding to make this: her little shenanigans and sexual rendezvous public knowledge. And shaming her would yield far greater results in getting her to quit than any legal pursuit would. I was able to wiggle my way out and break free from her dragnet.

...

She started soliciting action from me mere days after she first contacted me. That was, the following day after she had confronted Mira on the issue. Gosh, she smelled of breast milk for crying out loud. I thought we were bathing in the stuff. A Pretty little thing she was, and still is. I can easily see how she became Mrs. Kentise, so young and all. If pretty looks were everything. Then the man who had married her - Bob Kentise, would surely have gotten everything that the world has to offer the day he married her. But other than that? She's a dumbass nutcase and a freak. To be fair to her though. I can't help but think that she's got some real potential here because. For her to have gone and put together a scheme like that after finding out about her helper and me. And then use it to get some action back into her own partly retired sex life. After her husband had divorced her and remarried. Was border-line, genius. I believe someone sold her up short, somewhere along the way, her parents probably. She called me up the following evening after Mira gave her my contact information. Said it was important that I come to see her and get some things straightened out before she went to see her lawyer. Mira had already alerted me to what was up, so I was not the least bit surprised. I hopped into my car and trekked on over at the time appointed. Never did make much of the fact that Mira was not on the job there at the time. Mere coincidence? Or was it a result of careful planning? Anyway, I got there to find her home with her two children. The elder boy was home from school. And just like Mira had relayed it to me how it happened when she was called upstairs to meet with the mistress. It was basically the same setting. The laptop was there on the kitchen table, active and ready to go. On the screen, though, unlike how things were said to be in her rendition of the story. The screen wasn't facing the front where I could see it. I was bending my neck somewhat to try and sneak a peek whenever she wasn't looking my way but I still couldn't see anything.

"So," she said, "as it turned out, this is not the first time that you've been in this house, is it?"

"As a matter of fact, ma'am, it isn't, and I'm awfully sorry for my indiscretions and for trespassing - ma'am."

"So you're sorry? So you're sorry now? What makes you so sorry all of a sudden? Because you now find that you are facing some charges like trespassing on private property perhaps? Breaking and entering and, and..."

"Like I said - ma'am, I really am sorry, I meant no harm or disrespect. It was just a situation where..."

"A situation eh, that's what it was? A situation? So what can you say to me to make me not call the police right this minute and have you arrested?"

"I, I really don't know. I don't have anything to say other than to ask for your pardon ma'am. If you can find it in your heart to forgive me for this. I'm not a bad person or some evil person who has set out to do you, or anybody else harm. I just made a stupid mistake. It was a miscalculation of gigantic proportions on my part."

"A mistake eh, is that what this is? A mistake? Tell you what, let me think about it for a while, maybe run it by my lawyer and see what he thinks about the whole thing. Then we will decide where we go from there."

"I know I'm pushing my luck here ma'am but. Could you leave the lawyer part out for me? Please."

"No, you don't get to tell me what to do, or not to do here-mister. I'll do the telling around here. You should be thanking your lucky stars right now, as it is. That you have found me in a good mood or you would be negotiating with the cops by now."

By then the baby could be heard whining, and the boy, her brother, was a mama, mama-calling from the playroom next door. Her full attention was sorely needed elsewhere. "You may go now mister, but expect to hear from me again soon," she said.

"Thank you, ma'am, and have a good evening."

"Go, go."

So, I did just that, I got up and left.

...

Friday evening, almost exactly a week after that first meeting with Mrs. Kentise. As soon as I signed off from work at about five-thirty. The phone rang. It was the madam, for sure.

"I've got a proposal for you, Mister Manley," she said. "You need to get here as soon as possible." I point my nose in that direction. One can't afford to irritate any further this person on whom so much of one's future and freedom may depend, can he? She opened up the door to me, so I walked in.

"Have a seat," she said. As she turned the corner and went out of sight. I didn't sit, I could not. Instead, I scanned the room, just because. Wasn't looking for anything in particular. I was just uncomfortable. She came walking back into the living room, "sit, sit, sit down," she said. She spoke this emphatically but rather calmly and coolly. I sat down in the very first chair that my hand could reach at the table. She pulled out the chair on the opposite side of the table and sat down in front of me.

"Look," she said, "I've been thinking about a lot of things. I've come to the conclusion that you are who you say you are. Just someone who had made a stupid mistake and is awfully sorry for it. So..." She paused, pushed back the chair, and got up.

"I'm going to cut you some slack here," she said over her shoulder as she again turned the corner and went back in the direction of the room where she had gone before. Again, I snuck another peek around. Leaning towards the door that was slightly ajar, and which led into the children's playroom. It had come to my attention that I hadn't seen or heard anything of the children since I'd arrived there. Mrs. Kentise came back carrying the laptop. Or maybe it was another laptop in her hands. I can't say for sure which, but it was a laptop. She placed it on the table and hit the power button. With her right hand still on the backrest of the chair that she was about to pull out further. As she was about to sit back down, she paused in the middle of the act, leaning across the table at me.

"I think today is your lucky day," she said and then continued on to complete the act of sitting down.

After sitting back down and shaking herself comfortably in the chair. She began to manipulate the keys on the laptop. Progressively slowing down the act, "Hmm, hmm," she squeezed out several sounds of satisfaction. Of some sort of satisfying discovery, I think. Or something closely akin to it. For several minutes she was at it, leaving me there to wonder what she was up to. She must have found what it was that she was searching for because she shot me a lingering stare over the top of the angled-up computer screen. Then, she sat back in the chair and stared at me again. Slowly, her eyes narrowed, her lips parted as a thin grin began to birth itself out on her face.

"How about you give me some?" She asked as the grin widened on her face.

"Huh! What?" I reacted in puzzlement. The already wide grin she was wearing got bigger. As she slowly turned the screen towards me and...

Whoa. There I was, looking at, me, myself, and I. Right there on the screen, in the nude, with Mira. While standing there, in the presence of another woman, a strange woman. The one with whom I was not there at that time, in that state, to do, anything. Yet.

...

I slid the chair backward out from underneath the table. Turned slightly around to heave out. "I think it's time for me to go," I said.

"No, no, please," she begged, "I'm being genuinely straight-forward with you here, I don't want you to leave like this, not this time. Forget all that, that, that thing about the lawyer and all the rest," she said, and then, while pointing at the laptop, she added further:

"I really want us to do this, you and me."

"You really are sure about this?" I asked.

"Couldn't be 'surer,'" she replied. Her hands reached up and started to undo the buttons on the skimpy little sleeveless top she was wearing. She came walking over to where I was sitting as she finished up with the undoing of the buttons. Sat down edgily on my knees.

"Look." I said, "I've already done some things that I am regretting, and which is the very reason why I am here being quizzed and threatened by you. Am I going to regret this too? Coming here to talk to you?"

"No, that wasn't the reason why I called you here today, this is."

"I can't do this." I protested, "At least not with the threats of lawsuits hanging over my head."

"There are no lawsuits, there never was. Yes, I was angry and upset at first when I saw the recordings. Not even sure if it was at you, or Mira. I think it was more at her than at you, for bringing you in here but. When I started going through the recordings and got to see... all I wanted to do was to be in her place, in Mira's place. And I just knew that I had to give it a try. I'm really sorry for the back-handed methods that I might have used but. You wouldn't hold that against me, would you?"

While she spoke, she was undoing the buttons on my shirt. I gazed at the firm, full round breast there just bouncing and begging. I was just about to reach out and take hold and get a gluttonous bite out of em too but then I recalled that she was nursing. It's probably why they were looking so damn lush and inviting but I still would not take anything away from how beautiful the woman looked. The upper half of me, the sensible half: my head, my heart - to a lesser extent. And my mind told me to protest. Don't be drawn into this dragnet, this trap. But my lower half, my over-actively sensual half wasn't cooperating. He just wanted to hop on the horse and go a-giddy-upping down the tracks. Guess which half won out in the end? Yep that, you got it.

This dirty old puppy dog just hopped on in and went on riding along down the dead-end track. This was going to become a regular routine over the next little while for us. Every time that the kids go off to their daddy's place, she'd call, and me? I hop on over to their place, where me and... Mrs., Mrs. Jones, or was it Mrs. Ken? As in, Mrs. Kentise, yeah. Has got these red-hot chili peppers-like things going on. Until...

Libby came into the picture and spoiled everything, or did she?

While all this madness was going on with Mrs. Kentise and me. Mira and I were still having our regular rendezvous, only not at her workplace anymore. We never made that mistake again. So little by little, the heat started to wear out of the potful of Mrs. Kentise and me. Or so I wanted her to think of it. Mira likewise was seeing less and less of me.

"Is he getting tired of me?" She, Mira wondered this out while whispering in my hearing. But it wasn't that at all. In a way, Mira was deluding herself all the while into thinking that she and I were an item. I never did have much real interest in her from the start. Nothing beyond hitting the sack and burning some fat. If she was hoping and dreaming of something more than that. Then I guess one could call it a bonus. Everyone needs something to hold on to. A hope, a dream, in which case, I guess I'll always be her dream lover, won't I?

Libby stepped into the picture and everything changed. And no, I wasn't banging on her door. As you might be sitting there wondering even now. There was something different about the way I felt about her. I'd even seemed to have lost the desire for the "regular workouts" as I had grown accustomed to it up until then. That's when both Mira and Mrs. Kentise started turning to pester me: "Where are you? What are you up to? Why have I not seen you in x number of days?" And on it went like that. Until Mrs. Kentise was to have gotten the fabulous idea of going back to her old ways. Her old redundant threatening ways.

They call me Manley "The Techno man" for a reason. I am the go-to guy for all things technical in electronics in general and computers in particular but somehow. It would seem as if Madam Kentise did not inform herself well enough about who I was, to have known that part. So, when she changed from her threatening ways to start bedding down with me. I knew that that couldn't last. I didn't want it to last and by then. I had also managed to see enough of her to know that she could be a two-edged sword of sorts, cutting both ways. I had already tasted a bit of both bloody edges by then too. So I started to prepare myself for that day when she would turn again from sweet to bitter. So, I started to record our every encounter, like, our one-on-one conversations, and phone calls too. Well, her phone calls, not mine. Since I never did call her. Ever.

...

"Are you still f**king Mira?" The voice came yelling out in my ear.

"Wah... What... What?" I asked while rubbing away at lingering sleep and trying to pry my eyes open.

"Are you still f**king around with that girl, Mira?"

"I cannot see how who I may or may not be f**king around with is any of your business."

"Well, you must be f**king her. Or God knows who else, why you don't want to f**k me. And if you aren't getting it here, you must be getting it somewhere else, so who is it? Tell me, tell me."

"So, you mean to tell me, you call my house at 2:30 AM to inquire as to who I am f**king and why I'm not f**king you? Well, it looks like you're spot on right in at least half of the equation here. I'm not f**king you, and that is because I don't want to be f**king with you ever again. I never wanted to at the start, and I sure don't want to now, so go get a life and stop bothering me Ms. Kentise, I mean, Mrs. Addasa Kentise."

I hung up the phone and tucked my head back under my pillow. Straight away, the phone started ringing again. "What now?" I answered.

"You hang up on me madder f**kka, are you crazy? Do you know who you are f**king with? do you have any idea who you are f**king with?"

"Do you want an answer to those questions?" I asked. "Or is it that you just want to go a-rattling on? If I were you though, I would slow down and listen. Because I too have got some things to say which may be beneficial for you to hear, and since you have done got me wide awake and alert now, I might as well tell you. You've got your own choices to make here when I'm done. What you want to do with the information I am about to divulge is all up to you."

"I have been recording you, I mean, our every encounter is on tape. From meetings at your house to phone calls. And yes, even this last one and the ones before that, and all of those one-on-one conversations too. Listen to this.... Now, as you can see for yourself, or hear. It's all here. Everything is on record, and might come in handy someday don't you think - Mrs. Kentise? I mean, Mrs. Addasa Kentise pardon me."

"You slimy Son-of-a-bitch," she said.

"No ma'am," I replied, you ain't know nothing about me or my mother. Or anyone else on my family tree for that matter. So, don't you go about comparing me to whatever it is that your idea of a family is, or ought to be.

"What are you going to do with those recordings?" She asked.

"Nothing, nothing at all. Unless you make it worth my while to use them, then, and only then will I use them, and not necessarily in ways like you'd used the info you have on me. You see, I don't want to be doing you so I won't need to blackmail you into my bed, and I don't think that the threats of lawsuits will be time well spent for me. I want the biggest bang for my buck. So, how about me making all of your actions and shenanigans become public knowledge by circulating them, starting in your community, in the chosen places such as your worship temple? Your sports club and community center? And yes, I can make it all happen. I'm the Techno-Man remember?"

"You are a dead man, Manley. Or man "lie," or whatever the hell it is that your name is."

"That also is recorded for future reference, just in case. Remember, as I've already told you, I've been recording every bit of our encounters?" She hung up, why am I getting the feeling here that this is the end of her ever calling to bother me again?

Chapter Four: Your Mama is Calling You-Man.

The phone rang, and the call came bursting in on me, while on my drive back home from Mira's. It was Mama calling again. She said that she was wondering what had happened to me, and wanted to know if everything was okay. "How come you haven't come home as yet?" She inquired. She further wanted to know what "other mother" I might have that she doesn't know about.

"Oh! That? It's my other mother from another era," I said. "None other than Ms. Brodbendt from my primary school days."

Ms. B was calling for me, again. Ms. Brodbendt seems to think of herself as my mother and has always treated me like a son. Bubbles was to butt into my conversation again here like he's always done: "Yeah, a son-eh? Right," he said.

Ms. Brodbendt was the headmistress at Sunnyside School. That was the place where I was to have transitioned from a shy and insecure little Mama's boy to become one of the most feared. Bad-ass dudes, ever. That was after I was done fixing Bobbie Nooks' business with a busted head and a bloody face. The girls then came calling. And I? I was to have transitioned even further to become, as it was common to refer to dudes like me in those days: the girls' delight, "the girls dem sugar," and more, you name it. They have it. And after more words started getting around that I'm a no-nonsense-taker, girls-heartbreaker, and the despicable, girls them (dem) puppy dog, to name yet another few more that were popping up here and there on their list of names. My reputation was hitting the stars, both for the good and for the bad, but mostly for the bad. Man, I loved every minute of it.

Ms. Brodbendt kept me over the following afternoon because I was to have gotten sent off to the office for a fight with Bobbie Nooks. This was then followed up by another incident between Mrs. Taylor and me in class. Mrs. Taylor wanted a two-thousand-word essay on the virtues of a good education. Which she reminded me, "That is what you are here for, have it, (the essay,) have it on my desk first thing tomorrow morning," she said. I was being punished for the inattentiveness of my ways and for boisterous and disruptive behavior in class as well as other places on school grounds. She said further that I needed to focus more on the things that matter in life. "The things that 'really' matter."

I should have been more careful to put the pictures in an envelope before placing them in my notebook, but. You know! They were meant for her eyes only. Of course, I did the assignment. Two thousand words she had said. But it was Mrs. Taylor herself who'd imparted to us, all of us in her class mere days earlier that a picture is worth a thousand words. Well, she's now in possession of not two. But three of my finest selfies ever, in the nude of course. What else did you expect? The extra picture was intended as a bonus, just for her. Just for the fun of it. Well, there was more to my plan than what was to meet the eye. A method to the madness one might say. The pictures fell out of the folder and to the floor in front of the entire class when she'd popped open the notebook, she'd picked up off of the desk in front of me. No, I did not bother to place it on her desk first thing in the morning as she had asked of me. If I did all of that work to get it to her. The least that she could do was pick it up off the desk in front of me. Right? Maybe she was somewhat peeved by that and therefore did not exhibit the usual grace, charm, and caution when she'd popped it open.

"Whoa!" the whole class exclaimed as they all buoyed up and became instantly interested in the business of learning. More so in this than in what Mrs. Taylor was teaching. This surely did seem to conform more to their idea of what learning was about, to them. If only they could be made to become so stimulated by the prospect of seeing an

"A" or A-plus beside their names on the end-of-term exam papers. But yes, you know where this is going to lead me. Right? Straight to my most favored place in the entire world. My teenage world: the most principalest officette of them all... miss Brodbendt's office. Mission accomplished. That, as you might have already figured out, wasn't the beginning of my encounters with Miss B and her office. And it sure as hell wasn't going to be the last.

Ms. Brodbendt sat me down that evening and talked to me. Trying to figure me out, this I'd assumed. She'd concluded that I needed more and better adult supervision. She also said that, with proper guidance, I could indeed become a fine young man. She promptly offered herself up to "keep a close eye on me."

Mom's blessings were always one of those most valuable commodities for one to have around these parts. As it would apply to me and all her children. But something that was never very easily obtained. She must have okayed the headmistress' interventionist schemes though because off to Ms. Brodbendt's care, her office, and to her home, I ended up going. Although it was not on as regular a basis as I would have liked, it was regular enough. As it turned out, that was to be the beginning of something wonderful between the headmistress and me.

It started out quite innocently indeed. With some special sessions between her and me, like, time spent in her office. At other venues on or off school premises, they became more and more jovial and light-hearted as time went by. I even started to look forward to it, imagine that! I'm now looking forward to going to the principal's office. Hmm! Then she took it a step further, home, we went to her very own home.

Ms. Brodbendt lived alone in her fabulous home on the waterfront on Montreal's West Island. A two-story brick on top of a cut-stone house on a grass-covered woodland mound off Lakeshore Road. A property that mounts up straight out of the riverbed. She didn't have to ask me home more than once. I was in, for the long haul. Ms. Brodbendt's home quickly became my favorite place to be. And then, she just as quickly became my favorite person to be with, for a thousand more reasons than one.

She'd said that she's got something to do that evening that would require my helping hand. I obliged. What's not to like about helping Ms. Brodbendt? She was by then my most favored person in the whole wide world, after my mother of course. I was even taking to calling her mom by then. So mom, as it turned out, wanted to nurse her newborn (or more like, newly found) baby-me, into what her idea of a fully developed and rounded young man should be. If one is to care for the baby? Then one must start at the beginning. With the very basics. And that was just where she was to have gotten it all started, right there, in the mammary regions. Yes. She "babied" me.

...

"You just sit back and relax," she said. "There isn't much for you to do today really. I just want to have a little chat with you about a few minor subjects."

"No, no," she protested when I headed towards the single chair in a far corner of the living room. She then picked up a pillow off the large leather sofa. Fluffed it around in her hands, like this. Then with just as much care and tenderness. She propped it up in the left corner of the leather couch. Pat it again with her hands. "Sit, sit," sit she said. "Make yourself comfortable. Want something to drink? Help yourself. I helped myself as it had become as normal and regular as anything else of late for me to just help myself to whatever it was that I wanted to eat or drink, whenever I was at any of Ms. Brodbendt's places. Be it in her office at school or as it now is, in her home. I helped myself to a glass of iced tea and a handful of Ritz biscuits. I sat back down rather nimbly on the couch. Not wanting to spill any of the biscuits or the drink droppings on the floor, or worse, on the couch.

I could hear the shower going from behind the bathroom door. Ms. Brodbendt was taking a shower. In plain earshot of me sitting there in her living room. Imagine that. Yes, my overgrown, over-sensitized teenage boy's imagination started running as wild as Bigfoot the ape-man. Upon the suspicion that one of those humanoid kinds was venturing into his roaming territory, perhaps. And then, that's when

Bubbles spoke up again: "You're the principal man, Manley," he said. "She wants to do you-buddy!"

"Be off with you Bubbles," I said. "You're not real."

"Hey, which red-blooded teenage boy doesn't want to do his rather beautiful and charming schoolteacher?" Bubbles wanted to know.

"You're looking at him."

"Really? Tell me you don't secretly fantasize about knocking up Ms. Brodbendt? Or even that sassy little eye-treat of a form teacher of yours? If I were you though, I'd settle for the principal, because you ain't never going to get on the inside of Mrs. Taylor's pants. Not now, not ever." I couldn't argue with the bugger on those points. Not so much because I didn't know the answers to his queries. But even more so out of realizing that: incredulous though it might have seemed-all of that! Bubbles was right. "You know me just a little too well-B." I cautioned the little annoyance but... "We're going to have to do something about you. And soon."

Ms. Brodbendt came back into the living room wearing what looked like pajamas to me. A rather warm and cozy-looking pink panther jumpsuit sleepwear. With a long zipper in the front that ran all the way down from under the throat to just about the groin area, yes, right there. And a fluffy puppy dog-headed, black-nosed, red-tongued bed slippers on her feet. The large round friendly-looking black and white insert served as the ever-shaking shaky eyes of the "puppy-shoe." It seemed to be watching me from wherever in the room they were at any given point in time.

"I spoke to your mother again this afternoon," she said. As she re-enters the living room. She walked past me and headed towards the kitchen. Reached inside the cupboard for a wine glass, and then another.

"Would you like to try something a little different? Something a bit more mature than iced tea?"

"I, I don't know if I should do that. I've never had anything stronger than that before. I mean, iced tea. Well, I mean, not really. I did manage to down a beer or two once or twice before, but... um, what are you offering?"

She didn't bother to answer. She just poured the liquor in both glasses. Picked them up and came back towards the couch where I was sitting, handed me one of the glasses, then went and sat down at the other end of the couch.

"Don't gulp it down," she said. "Take your time, sip it, and savor the flavor." I was watching her closely though indirectly. She stirred the drink around with one finger, rolling the ice cubes in circles around the glass. Then she licked it, her finger, and shook the glass in a circular motion. The ice in the liquor was making a clinking, rattling sound in the glass. I shook my glass in somewhat of a similar manner. Or as close to it as I could get. I didn't stick my finger in though, I lifted the glass to my lips and took a tiny sip. Held it in my mouth for a little while and then slowly swished it around in my mouth and all over my tongue. After confirming that it was not a bigger bite than I could chew, I swallowed it. Not bad, I thought. Not bad at all. I took another sip, holding it for longer. Long enough to really taste the flavor this time. I noticed the hint of sweetness and a slight tingly feeling on my tongue, I swallowed. And felt the warmth within.

"As I was saying," she continued. "I spoke to your mother earlier this afternoon. She said that she has noticed the changes in you and is quite happy with the improvements. She seems to think that I've got something to do with it and wants you to spend more time with me."

While talking, she reached up for the zipper head and pulled it down a couple of inches. Then shuffle her body into a more comfortable position. Lift her legs up onto the couch and place them one over the other between us. The bottom of the puppy dog shoes is now right in front of my face every time I look around. Which was, like, constantly.

"Do you like the drink?" She asked while pulling down the zipper head yet further.

"It's, it's okay," I mumbled this and took another sip. I wanted to quit and split right there and then. But no, I had to protect my rep.

"What rep?" Asked Bubbles. I rebuked him, from within. The big black fluffy meowing pussy cat came hobbling over and hopped up onto her knees. Its butter-like, buttonhole eyes were busily watching me with suspicion, while she,(Ms. Brodbendt,) gently stroked its head. Smoothing out the furry fluff. I would surely like to be stroking her pussy cat too. But. I ain't that lucky it would seem.

She'd picked up the lazy-looking bundle of fur. Bedding it out on top of her arm and supported it by the plump roundness of the breast against the pink bunny jumpsuit. She got up and went back into the kitchen. Carrying her pussy, yes, the fluffy ole cat along with her. I suppose it was to replenish the glass. Didn't wait long enough to find out. I took the opportunity at that point to bolt into the washroom. By then, I had some very urgent teenage boy types of issues to tend to, and fast. My teenage boy's mind had suddenly started to wonder. Am I here hinged on paranoia?

Everywhere I looked around I'd see, weird piercing eyes staring back at me, from the fake puppy dog shoes to the furry overweight pussycat sitting on her knee, it was like the whole blinking house was a-watching me, though I'd much rather be busy, cuddling up with Miss B. If ever, I am to be found "cuming" to Ms. Brodbendt's home on any type of a regular basis. I'd figured that: we, meaning me. Myself, and I? We're going to have to do something about this wretched old pussy cat. No?

Chapter Five: Close Your Eyes and Sleep Pretend.

It came about on this particular evening when I had to drop her (Libby) home because Kamal had gotten himself involved in an accident with his car and another vehicle on the way while driving into town to pick her up. It wasn't a total write-off, but the car had to be towed to a repair shop. Kamal himself was not injured. Other than for injured pride, perhaps that, yes, he was quite a bit shaken up in that regard.

He'd called to inform Libby of the accident and advised her to take the train or get a taxi home. I happened to have been sitting right there next to her when the call came in. "No need for the train or cabbies I told her, I'll take you home." Of course, she protested.

"I can't let you do that," she said, "this is not your responsibility."

"Is this your brother's, Kamal's responsibility, and his only? And who made it out to be so, who was it that decides that: nobody must ever take you home except for your brother?"

"No, no, it's not like that, it's just that I have never done it before. I mean, Kamal has always been the one who drives me to school and back. No one else has ever done that, and I hardly ever ride the bus nor have I ever taken a taxi. Except for my dad's car, of course. He's a taxi operator you know?"

"Well." I said, "Today is your lucky day, sort of. I mean, I'm neither a cabbie nor do I operate the bus but I will get you home, safely."

...

The rush hour traffic was as it has always been-slow. We went along with the flow. Libby took the opportunity in the slow-moving traffic to venture into telling me more about herself and the family. Kamal, she said, was having a hard time with his newly wedded wife. "They'd gotten married just over a year ago. And immediately went to work aunting me up." They're now expecting their second child but all is still not well with them. Selma had arrived from India for the expressed purpose of marriage to Kamal. It was an arrangement. "She's quite a good and decent girl. A proper homemaker and all. But Kamal is still not satisfied with her, it would seem. He said she doesn't know how to please a man. I suppose that means sexually," she added. "Said that she's old-fashioned and boring. The problem is, he hasn't been able to articulate the trouble he has been having with her in a way that could make Dad and Mom understand why he seemed to be so unhappy ever since he has gotten married."

"But he tells you this?"

"Yes, he tells me everything. We have always had a good and open line of communication like that, Kamal and me."

While she talked on, she was playing toss-up with my right hand. She'd picked it up off the transmission shift lever and thereafter virtually claimed it as her very own. For the entire duration of the drive from downtown Montreal to her house on the West Island, it was hers. The golden setting sun on the horizon makes her face seem encircled by a halo every time I turn around and look at her. She'd picked up my hand, my right hand, and placed it palm-to-palm in her left hand. Then covered it over with her right hand. As we talked, she would work on the hand, from tossing it up and down, patting it, and rubbing it, onto interlocking fingers. Both hers and mine. Finger to finger. She rests my hand on top of her leg at the point of the knee but as time went by. It slowly inched all the way up her thigh and soon it was right there in the groin area. She was absentmindedly tracing her fingers all over my hand. She then ran her finger over my fingernails. That's when he spoke up again. Yeah, Bubbles, that was when I heard him say: "Hey, check this out, she's checking for jagged edges - dude, you'd better not be flunking on the manicure routine thing..."

Before long, my hand and fingers were working on tracing the inner thigh, and she noticeably signed off the radio dial - her radio dial. The conversation slowed. Her eyes closed; her head tilted backward to hit the headrest on the seat. Her lips parted. Gradually, the gate opened and closed, opened, and closed. Then opened again, wider. Then it closed, opened, and stayed open. I moved in slowly and slid into her hot, throbbing wetlands. "Ahhh..." She exhaled, covered her mouth with the back of her hand, and bit on the knuckle of the arched middle finger. Bubbles again chimed in: "Yes mi fren, mi good fren, we back a street again." He started chirping in my inner ear.

"Don't you start that shit again," I said, in my inner voice.

...

Was it her own idea, or was that their parents' hands there at work? Still, trying to control her at twenty-four years of age? The latter is my best bet.

Kamal and I arrived at the family home at almost the same time. He drove home the delivery cube truck from the store. Said that the car would still be in the garage for a couple of days yet, to get the repairs done. I pulled the car up behind the truck that had just pulled up and parked minutes before we (Libby and I) got there. Libby did point the truck out to me during the drive-in. While we were still on St Charles Boulevard on the route coming in. It was just before they turned onto another street leading to their house off Brunswick Boulevard when we stopped and parked. "Look," she had said, "that's our truck, Kamal must be using it as a replacement for the bang-up car." She was right.

"Who's this person?" Kamal wanted to know before I even got out of the car. I'd stopped the car alongside the truck and was positioning myself for a parallel park. But before I could begin backing up, Libby wanted to get out and quiz her brother about what had happened. With the accident and all.

"Kamal - this is my friend, Manley," she chirps.

"What kind of a friend are you?" He asked right off the cuffs.

"Hi Kamal, I'm Manley, Libby's a friend of mine, and I'm mighty happy to meet you. I've heard a lot about you, and would sure like to get to know you a bit better too."

"What kind of friend are you to my sister?" He asked again while quickly pulling back the hand after taking, and shaking mine.

"We're the kind of friends who happen to meet and sometimes share a chat over a meal at school, and..." This was getting way too uncomfortable for me. So I bade them farewell and parted... We were to meet again though.

Chapter Six: Do It for the Love

… I would kill myself if they ever tried to do that sort of thing to me, Libby said. While she was sharing the story of Kamal and Selma with me.

"Don't talk like that Libby." I rebuked her, "You shouldn't go around saying things like that."

"But it's true, I mean it. What kind of life is that? Living your whole life with someone who you don't even like, let alone love? Just because your parents think they know better than you what is good for you? They may do it to Kamal and get away with it. But that's as far as they're going to get with those old-fashioned rituals unless they decide to go back to the baby pit for another child to practice on. Not Libby, though, thank you very much."

"Don't you think that people can find happiness within an arranged marriage, ever?"

"Good for them if they do, but not for me. I'll go find my own dream-lover with no help from anyone."

"You know, I should be really thrilled to hear that kind of talk coming from you. Since it would seem like I don't stand a snowball's chance in hell of your folks choosing someone like me, for their daughter. But I can't help but feel a bit concerned about you taking this stance."

"I'm a big girl, I can fend for myself." She defended herself. "You don't have to go about worrying about me."

"…Is this the way it works in your household?" I asked her later on. "You have got to pass every exam that you sit?"

"Why else would I sit them, if not to pass them?" She blurted back at me.

"There are people in this world, you know, people who believe and will swear on their mother's grave to the fact that one can learn an awful lot more from failure than success. Or at least, from failing an exam. As it is in this particular case here rather than from passing one. You know, failure tends to get one to put things into proper perspective sometimes and to try harder the next time. And then, one might even be able to pick up on a thing or two that one might have missed on the first take."

"I would much rather pass it on the first take and be done with it, thank you. Which, by the way, is exactly what I'm expecting to happen this summer. I just want to be done with this and be out of here. The sooner I'm out, the better."

"And why is that? Don't you like it here? Or is it somebody else that you can't stand to see anymore? Me perhaps?"

"No, no, this is not about you. I just think it's time for me to start moving on with my life. To start doing my own thing, in my own way."

"So what, or who is preventing you from doing your own thing now as it is?"

"Can we change the subject? Please? I don't want to get into that sort of thing now. Maybe someday in the future, but not now."

"Yes, I was married before," I told her in response to her queries as to my marital status, or more like, as to why a nice guy like me is not. You know, like? Married? "I got hitched at twenty-six years of age. That marriage lasted for four years. In fact, we were together for only three of those four years when she was to have up and left, and a year later, we were divorced. She found someone else. Someone who just happened to have had much more money than I did. So, she started acting up. Behaving weirdly and blaming me for anything and everything. Then, I was to have committed the biggest faux pas ever, when I gave her a cheap gift I had picked up at the pawnshop on her birthday. That's all I could afford at the time or barter trade for, but it's the thought that counts. Right? She said she needed space. It wasn't long afterward though before that space was nicely filled by someone else, someone who just happened to be her brother's best friend and co-worker. They were both jockeys riding at the Woodbine racetrack at the time and were locked tight in an epic and fierce battle to become the top jockey of the year. Needless to say, the money was rolling in in that arena. Coincidence or what? Little buggers weren't just riding horses though. They were riding bitches too."

"Ugh!" Libby gasped. "Are you serious? I can't believe you just said that."

"Bitches as in dogs you know? You know, these competitive sports professional types?" I said further, lying through my grinning white teeth. "They just seemed to delight themselves in spending time and money on extra-curricular, extra-judicial activities, such as those that cannot face the light of a Sunny day," I said all of that still continuing along in the deceit, trying to deter her from the real and original meaning of what she knew darn well that I was saying. She wasn't fooled, that's for sure.

"Yeah, right," she said.

Chapter Seven: Techno-man, Something's Wrong Here

I was going on a work-related trip the following evening. Got a gig to get to at the techno center. To repair computers and systems. What awaited me there was to become an issue later. The madam was alone in her office. I didn't know that at the time. Not until I arrived on the ninth floor and walked the long passageway that leads to nine hundred and twenty-six and wrapped on the door.

"Come on in, the door is unlocked," the voice came to me through the front door. I turned the latch on the door and pushed it open.

She was sitting there at her desk. She seemed all steeped in a hodge-podge of paperwork. But at the same time, she was wrapping up a call on the telephone line. She stuck up a well-manicured finger and mouthed off the words; "give me a minute." Then she pointed to the sofa, "Have a seat," she again mouthed off the words at me. I didn't bother to sit, I just glanced at my wristwatch. She got the message, I'm sure, she's bright. The managerial-business-type that she is and all. She knows the value of time. She did not get up from the desk and walked over to take my hand that I'd offered, as would have been proper.

"Manley," I said while extending a ready right hand in greetings.

"I know," she said, "I know who you are, and why you are here. Let's get to it shall we?" She spoke further as she handled the mouse and foray through a series of clicks on the computer.

"This thing needs some urgent attention," she said. "We'll get to it in a second. "Just give me a moment, let me close these here and then, clean up this mess."

"Take your time," I said, "I've..."

"There, all done. Come around this side." She directed me to the right side of her desk,

"...where you can see more clearly."

She pushed back the swivel chair slightly. Leaning back in her seat. Both elbows resting on the side armrest. Her purple nails, polished shine, and in sync with her earrings, eyeshadow, and lip gloss. Swayed to the rhythm of her shaking hands and feet. She looked me over, in a quick and sweeping analytical scan. Then she looked me square in the eyes.

"Are you going to just stand there? Or did you come here to work? Come on, come over here."

In utter puzzlement, I questioned this. "Are you going to be sitting there while I work?" I asked this across my pointy indexed finger, straight at her, sitting there in that comfy leather chair of hers. "I can't... I don't work like that, ma-am."

"Well, I'm going to be needing to show you what you need to do here - won't I?" She chided me quite sternly. I inched my way around the desk via the far side and voila...

There she was, looking rather regal. Leaning further back in her seat now. With her chest protruding forward in confidence, her well-tailored navy blue jacket opened down the front. Obediently laying smooth over the white cotton blouse. The topmost button on the blouse was already undone. Even though the cut was already too low, to begin with, for modesty, or even for one to be referring to it as "the topmost button." It wasn't anywhere near the top of those, and that. On her feet, the shoe heel of the purple and black spike heel shoe she wore was long and so thin that I winced somewhat. At the mere thought that someone would even try to walk in them. Her legs crossed, the shoe on the top, (or crossover leg,) was just dangling there from her toes. While the shoe heel tilts downward. And hung there shaking with her every move below her own heel, and the arched sole of her foot. I couldn't help myself. I had to take a second lingering glance at the cleavages. Look! Wow!

On the far side of where I was standing to the right of her, the generous peel away of the blouse from the left breast. Allowed for a sumptuous serving of eye treats dangling at me, even down to the darkened round circle somewhere around the nipple. But the nipple herself seemed like she was too shy to come all the way out of the closet. Or maybe she was downright mean, she stayed hidden from view, however she could.

My business card reads "Techno Manley-For all things computers. From hardware to programming and software to design. Call us. We'll get your system up and running in no time."

No, I did not forget about that part. I would have made some mentions in all of these descriptions of her upper bodily attire and even the foot on down to the footwear, but not from the waist down. That is because, there was nothing there, nothing other than for the faint marks where the stockings had anchored itself onto the upper thigh not too long ago. Probably just before I walked in there.

"Like what you see?" She asked cheekily.

"How did you find out about me? I mean, how did you get a hold of my contact info?"

"Are you operating on some closed level? Like, like a private net-work or something?" She shot back at me. "Your business cards and adverts are everywhere, with information on everything about you and what you do, and your profile is prominently featured on LinkedIn. And yes, that's where I got it, - satisfied?"

"No, no, that's not how I roll, you've got the wrong guy here. I don't work like that," I said. Pointing my nose back in the direction from whence I had come, I headed for the door. "I hope you will find the right person to get your system up and running again." I said this over my shoulder while I was leaving, "Sorry I was not able to help you out here."

Me: Reaching for the doorknob, I turned around to say, "I know someone who..." hoops.

I was just in time to catch a glimpse of the spike-heeled shoe as it zipped past my head, long before I'd even managed to duck out of the way. It crashed into the door and bounced back to the middle of the open space in front of the desk.

Me: "Take very good care of yourself-miss." I pulled the door open and tried to squeeze through to get out.

Just then, her right hand went down. As the left leg heaved itself upward to meet up with the violent, ready-to-launch-another-attack right hand. I bet she was reaching for the other shoe.

Almost in sync with the click of the lock on the closing door, came the big bang. And then a thud and a rattle. I was right, I bet she'll be picking up a pair of purple and black spike-heel shoes off the floor, somewhat damaged. Before clearing out of the office later today.

Me: Waiting for the elevator to get out from there, while I was standing in the hallway. I ran my finger through my hair and wondered out loud, "What the hell just happened? Has someone been flying over the Koo-Koo's nest of late? When, and how did I get to such a place as this? Where I'm now scampering away from such a ready and willing, no-stress, no-frills-attached Sex Fest?"

And that's when Bubbles spoke up again: "So what's preventing you from just turning around and going right back in there to finish off the job, the woman is still there you know, just as hot, wet, and ready as before." Who is Bubbles, you'd asked?

(Bubbles is my split personality, you know the type, that smart-ass voice inside who sometimes cracks wise-guy jokes just to piss me off. And then there are the odd moments when he talks sense into me.)

Me: "Will you just shut the f**k up." I rebuked him, Bubbles that is. But if you or anyone else was looking on, you might have thought that I was just someone who was going off the deep end talking to myself. Well, perhaps I am.

"You don't even know a rat's ass what you are talking about," I said. "Don't you know that a woman scorned is the best one to stay the hell away from? And this one right here? She's the Chief of them all. Everything about her spell's danger"

Bubbles: "Dangers are ever-present in the high-stakes games dude. And those are the ones that you love to play most? No? And frankly, they are the only ones that are worth your while playing - no? Where the focus of your attention is, that's what makes the difference, remember?"

Me: "I'm not afraid if that's what you're here implying, it's just that I haven't been thinking straight of late. I'm not quite sure what has come over me lately."

"Libby? Perhaps?" Interjected Bubbles again.

Chapter Eight: Women Are from Where Again?

Guess you could say that I've come full circle. As a small boy, I was just so damn shy and insecure. Afraid of everything and everyone. So much so that I could hardly get anything done. Grandma, first, and then mom. They were my only safe spots. My soft landings. I didn't like girls, I couldn't understand them, and I most certainly, couldn't stand them.

These women, though (and a few men too to a lesser extent) are the driving forces in my life. Other than for my mother and grandma who were the very first such influences on me. Ms. Brodbendt was the first one to have gotten my attention and captured my teenage boy's lustful thoughts, and imagination. This was to have happened at about twelve going on thirteen years of age. It was my fairy godmother, though, who initiated me into the real meat of the matter. A young woman with chestnut hair, and Amber eyes. Skin so soft and clean as if she'd never been bitten by a mosquito. Or even had a pimple or scar. Or maybe she was just over waxed, over-shine. Boy! She sure was smooth.

When I got back home after leaving the Millers, I discovered that she was gone. They told me that she had gotten herself a teaching job south of the border. And headed down to the great big USA. Making the big bucks by doing what she does best - teaching, for pay. Or was it? I can't help but wonder at times if she'd taken all of her teaching tools with her. Her tactics, and all of her good godly Gaddy techniques with her when she went down there, hmm. Some southern teenage boy must be counting his lucky stars right this minute.

...

My fairy godmother and her family were living just two blocks away from my mother's house. That's the house where we all were living at the time. My mother, my sister Amy, my brother Norm, and me. Too close to her leer for comfort as it was to turn out. But who's complaining? Not me. She, Gaddy, that's what I started calling her since no one seemed to know her name. Everyone else around those parts just calls her "Miss." So, Gaddy (or Miss,) was able to watch me as I grew up and developed. Putting on the muscles. Between the ages of thirteen and fifteen. I would have grown about a full foot in height, and I was putting on weight too, in all of the right places. And with pure clean muscles, needless to say. I was ripped. As for her? She noticed, for sure. She never did miss out on the opportunity to tell me how great I looked. I was beginning to get the feeling at times though, that someone was talking to her. Telling her things about me. About all of the trouble I was having or getting into at school. She started showing a bit too much interest in me. And in particular. In those personal and private aspects of my teenage life. Much too much for my comfort at the time. And then, she offered to come "sit with me, and talk to me." The timing couldn't have been wackier. It was just around those same times that I was beginning to get cozy in Ms. Brodbendt's company. I was to be seeing a spike in sexual tensions in that arena. Unlike it was to be with Ms. Brodbendt though. Gaddy didn't waste any time in priming and prepping me for the journey. She just delved right in with the brush and started painting. Shiue. This well and timely relieved puppy dog was to have breathed a huge sigh of relief. Not a minute too soon.

...

Unlike how things were at home, in our house. There were never more than four people living there at any given time. My fairy godmother, in contrast, seemed to have an entire village living in their apartment. She was always reminding me that, she's from a very big family. Her family is big alright. It's so big, in fact, that. She has two sisters with the very same name. The big joke in the family is this: their mother has got so many children that, she'd forgotten that she had already used up that name. And since the other sister, the one whose name it was at the first, had also got a pet name by which she was commonly known. They didn't bother to change anything. Everybody just went along with the flow. They all knew very well who's who: Deloris number one (Dell) and Deloris number two. Was born almost a full decade apart. So, there was never an issue in deciding which "Deloris" was which. With all of that crowded mess, though. It was only a matter of time before somebody was going to get in somebody's way. Or trip over somebody, and fall.

It came about on one of our, by then, regular rendezvous. I went over to her house. At her invitation, of course. She'd said she would be home alone that day. Our house was the meeting place of choice up until that point. But for some strange reason. I was beginning to get somewhat uncomfortable with the whole idea of carrying my girlfriend into my mother's house. No. Wait a minute, she was not a girl. So, "girlfriend" is probably not the correct term here. She was my female friend. This was a grown-ass woman, not a girl. I had gotten to the point where I was getting uncomfortable with the practice of carrying her over to our place, and into my mother's house whenever she was not there. And for no other purpose or reason than to make out with her in the basement. I'd made my over-sensitized hang-ups and reservations on the matter known to Gaddy. And she agreed with me that, it didn't seem right. Said that her mother would have been pissed off too if she should discover that she, or any other of her siblings should ever do that sort of thing. But then, not many days later, she did just that. She invited me over, on the lot. Said she was going to be home alone. I hopped right on over and wasted no time in getting into the planned activities of the day: working on the day shift one might say. In the middle of it, without any prior warnings. Her little sister would have popped right in and disrupted the apple cart. To her great credit, though, she didn't tarry. Just turned around on her heels and headed straight back out. Maybe, I thought. Maybe that was the norm in that household, hmm. That was it for me though, I was done. You could fold me up and wring me out like a wet rag after that, and hang me on a clothesline somewhere. I was that much "done." L'il Sissie was not done though. As for her, she was just about to get started. She wanted in on the action, and fast. I think this little encounter, did feature prominently in Gaddy's decision to go south when the opportunity arose a year or two later. The relationship between her and her little sister also took a beating from that moment on. As for me? In the meantime, I was majoring in running. Running out of places for us to get comfortable and get down. Running out of interest in Gaddy and the family gang. Running into some other new and interesting prospects, here and there. Running away from home. Running headlong into Mrs. Miller, and then…

What? Did you ask if I did do them crazy little things with l'il Sissie too? What kind of a question is that - Boo?

…

My mom used to boast a lot in those days when talking about me. Telling tales about how kind and caring her little boy (me, big bulky strapping old me,) was. She'd said that I would take the shirt off of my back and give it to a friend in need. The truth is though. I'd take off not only the shirt but the pants. The underwear too, and even down to the holey socks off my feet for others. And they didn't even have to be my friends. Just someone who has got the proper motives. The proper desires, and the proper rewards for my ever-in-demand services. Or simply, just someone who will ask, nicely. I've always been sweet and kind like that. Ever willing and ready to help out someone in need. And dad?

…

My father was a Rolling Stone. So they say. Never stayed long enough in any one place to be able to get comfortable with the place. Or with himself being in that place. Mom's favorite words in referring to him in those days were, "a sperm donor." She said that he was nothing more than a sperm donor. She'd also said that it seemed like every time he shook his pants. A child would fall out. As for him, he never did seem to miss out on a chance at shaking those damned pants. Whether it was to be in a dark shit hole somewhere. Or in some high and lofty places, shaking he would. He doesn't seem to have any idea as to how many children he has fathered so far by doing so. In real terms? He'd said that he had stopped counting at thirty-one. And that was several years ago. The significance of the thirty-one in his view? He can ascribe one to each and every day in any and every month of the year. My mom accounts for two of those children. I could never have understood why she hung around long enough to repeat "the mistake." But I'm kind of happy that she did. I really am mighty fond of my sister - Amy.

My mom did take yet another kick at the baby-making machine, long after our father had skipped the scene for good too. The result of that venture is our little brother - Norm. Short for: Norman Whitley. After dad was to have upped and left her with a three-month-old baby (me) and nothing with which to care for herself, and a young child. Mom had to fall back onto her own resourcefulness, and fast. I was shipped off to Grandma's place. While Mom returned to work. We were all still living in our mother country then. Our mother country of Jamaica. In the West Indies. When her second child came less than a year later. Grandma had to put her foot down firmly.

"Every woman," she said, "have a right to mind their own ill-begotten children." She was heard to have spoken this further. "I took care of my own children. With no help from anyone. And I'll be damned if I am going to take on any more of other people's responsibilities towards their own children, in my old age."

Of course, Grandma loved all her children. And that included this daughter too, (my mom). And all of her grandchildren, including Amy and me. She was not going to return me back home to my mother. Even if she could. "But not anymore," she had said. She was just disappointed and frustrated though, that's what I think. At the sort of choices that her daughter was making. But most of all, she was tired, simply tired.

It wasn't very long after those things that Grandma passed away. I was forced to go back to living with my mother and sister. I believe

Jack Whitley entered the picture because. Mom needed help with us. Being in a new country and all. And you?

We'd arrived in the new country of Canada. With little more than the clothes on our backs. And had was to start all over from scratch. The help Jack had promised was very timely. He seemed to her like water in a thirsty land at the time. The help though, that she ended up getting from the good old Jack, in real terms, was her third child and almost no more help than she did have before. Mom never did give old Jack a chance to do any further damage. By doing it to her again. He was out of the door like a stale fart against the rushing wind. She opened up the door, and then, just like that? He was gone.

...

So, like I was saying, I had some real trouble on the social scene as a small boy. I couldn't understand the girls. And boys? As for them. It seemed as if, the only thing that they would want to do with me then, was to beat me up. And that they surely did, at every juncture. And with every opportunity that was to present itself. I stuck to myself a lot back then. Until that day when Bobbie Nooks - the schoolyard bully, messed with me once too many times. I busted his head. I then kicked the living daylights out of his already bloody face and got sent to the principal's office for it. I got sent to the principal's office a lot in those days. To my mother's chagrin. But as for me, the more I get sent there, the more I get to love it. Why? Stay with us to learn more about it and other such things as we go along.

Nooks never did bother me again. And that wasn't the only strange thing that was to happen there that bloody day. The rest of that bunch of wolfhounds. That wild pack of sticky slime-dripping kids seemed to get the message loud and clear: don't you go a-messing with that Manley kid. He'll kick your face bloody. The most amazing side effect of it all though, as it was to have turned out. Was to come about in the way the girls started to look at me and treat me from then on. It was like night and day, the difference. Suddenly, they wanted my company and wanted to be with me. Some even "wanna do me," including Bobbie Nooks' girlfriend - Jada. Strange indeed. Seems to me like some girls only want to be with the big bad wolf in the pack. The ones who will hear, see, and eat them raw. Like me. I was still afraid of that part though. I never quite knew what to do, really. Or even how to do it, right up until…

My fairy godmother would have shown up with her training gloves on. And started showing me everything that I needed to know. By practice and all. She, like Ms. Brodbendt before her. Was starting to invade my teenage boyhood imagination with the wonders of sex and sexuality. She'd happened to have bumped into me and promptly began filling in the missing links. Those that were sprouting up between Ms. Brodbendt and me, but were not being fulfilled, yet. She then ventured into filling in all the blanks. Not a moment too soon. She was a teacher too, working at another school at the time. Separate and apart from the one I was attending. But she lived close enough to our house, to my mother's place, to be very convenient. And that's all I'm going to say about her on this particular point. In order to protect the innocent. I gave them both what they wanted though, the two of them, at some other odd points in times, even three. All in my own "sweet darling" way.

According to (Gaddy,) my fairy godmother. If I'm going to be anything remotely resembling what a man ought to be. There are some things that I need to know and fast. More or less the same as what Ms. Brodbendt had said, so. She too would have volunteered her services. And then, what I became, what I turned out to be, is probably the very reason why I'm in this shithole of a situation today. Words started getting out and around me. And just as quickly it was to have exploded out of all proportion. Gossip talks, name-calling, and reputation building. And then…

My fairy godmother waltzed right on in. Literally picked me up, and put me on top of the girl from next door, I can't even remember her name now, but then. Just like the good school teacher that she was. She coached me along. She was coaching both of us along. I wasn't quite sure at times if my practice mate was enjoying the ride or abhorring it. But she was in it, in all of those agonizing ways. Well, agonizing on my side of the leger that is. As it turned out, Gaddy my fairy godmother, didn't seem to think that it was all that it was supposed to be. Practicing with the girl from next door, because. She, not many days later. Was venturing to do it all by her fabulous self - the coaching. Practice, show, and tell everything. And boy, what a teacher, mentor, and coach she turned out to be. I was never the same again.

Chapter Nine: Amy's Lost and Found.

It was an unholy meetup. Although it was happening right there in the holiest of places: in church. She was recovering from something. Something that was to leave her with visible as well as audible scars... And he, he was recovering from something too, something somewhat of a different sort, like, a scarred past. Most of which cannot face the light of day. But he has a heart of gold or more like, a heart like the diamonds. A diamond heart, perhaps. As a matter of fact, many folks said that it was the pressurized process that he had been through and had managed to survive. That was what had brought him to his current state of being. And make him out to be the ever-so-in-demand person he had managed to become.

Gervis was a master musician (among other things.) He was also a devoted worker in the church. He has been, in recent times, rising up the holy ladder of ministry to become the secretary-treasurer for the men's fellowship department. He was mentoring boys to become better men. Better husbands, and better fathers.

Brother Gervis was fast becoming an icon and a staple in the church. The women revered him, including my mother and my sister Amy. Most of the young women just wanted to get their claws into him. Including my sister Amy. Folks said that it was those women who were to have drawn him into the church, chiefly my sister Amy. That's what the women in my bloodline always seemed to do. They go off to church, dragging their male folks along with them, kicking and screaming, even. That was what mom did to her children. That's exactly what she did to me.

The very first chance that these selfsame male folks will get to get out of there though. That's what they usually do, just like me. That was exactly what I did.

We usually go off searching for other types of women folks. The types who are oftentimes ever so very delighted to go dragging us off into some other, much more fun direction. Doing much more fun things. Screaming yes, but not necessarily kicking. At least not as much nor as hard as we were before. These are the types of women folks who tend to get my mojo going, every single time. These are the types that I adore. If I love them? Yes, you've guessed it right, I do.

So, sister Mills was sitting in the front row seats. In terms of her getting the first pick at Brother Gervis. She was on top of the pile, so to speak. And therefore, she had the first pick at the lottery draw to get at him. In accordance with the theory. And so, she did just that. She'd ventured out to exercise her options, at the very first chance that was to present itself.

Brother Gervis was on the keyboard doing his usual thing - playing an interlude while the testimony service was dragging on. It was Sister Mills' turn to testify and she wasn't going to miss this opportunity to stake out her claim on the man. Sister Mills was a woman with a scarred beauty - yes. But she was a survivor too. She was recovering from cancer at the time, cancer of the throat. This was to slightly alter the tone of her voice but other than that, she was as classy as they come. Always immaculately dressed and well-spoken, other than for the tiny speech impediment. And she was always chauffeured around in her big Lincoln Town car, by her ever-so-loyal and attentive chauffeur - Gus. Also known as Angus, or is it the other way around the bus? What difference does it make? So then, she met up with this man who came to church. With scars of a different sort. Gervis was his name. Or was it Gervis who had met up with her when he did take to church life as a replacement for his previous tug life? Either way, Gervis was a man with a badly scarred past, but he has a heart of gold, and he is (at this point?) In the church. What Sis. Mills thought of him. Like, who she thought he was and what he was after, conflicted greatly with who he really was and what he was really after. She was into the finer things of life alright, and he? He was going about trying to refine things. Or just a couple of things that he thought were the only things that really mattered in life after all. He was out to save himself and his son. He wanted to remake himself and win full custody of his son. They, Brother Gervis and sister Mills. Ran into each other there in the church, she had been watching him for quite some time it would seem. Just like all of the rest of those women were, because. After an otherwise insignificant verbal exchange between them, where he had inquired into the cause of the neck scar, the inner thoughts, her inner thoughts which were there incubating inside her, seemingly. And the desires she had cherished for months, years probably. Those desires suddenly popped out like chicken from the hatch, and she ran with it. He followed along for a while. Trying to glean whatever insights he could garner on the inner workings of the minds of these sorts of members of the opposite sex. And to try and figure out what makes them function. His findings, and what little of it that can face the light of day, were, as could be expected, very controversial. To say the least. He had merely asked about the scar, how did she come to have them? She took hold of a microphone and ventured to announce that: "he wants to check me out." She then went on a show-and-tell episode. Baring her soul in what one might conclude was a misguided effort at winning the man. Will she? Let's see.

At this point, everyone sitting around was (seemingly,) interested in what was going on in front of them. He was sitting there at the piano. He was a brilliant musician, Brother Gervis was playing, dragging the others along, the other "not-so-good musician wannabes." But then came Sis. Mills, standing up for the right to speak again, and then, Brother G was gone. After he got up and left. Nobody wanted to hear any more of what was left of the "musicians" so they also split, one after the other. Until they were all gone.

So the question now is, why does a woman behave the way she does? And in particular, why did this one woman behave in that manner? And what effect did her behavior have on the real outcomes and on the schemes of such things? This versus a man's behavior in this and other such circumstances. Like, this one particular man's behavior and desire? The causes and effects of things one might say.

...

Gervis was a gangbanger of the worst kind in former times. Amy, my darling l'il sister was deep into him. That was after he was taken into the churched life. She has her whole heart set on winning him over. But unlike most of the other women who were out to get him. She was taking things really slowly indeed. She had already broken one of the church's cardinal rules once before, when she went out and got pregnant, out of wedlock. And she didn't want to go repeating and reviving the sin monsters. Amy was in college at the time when she was to have gotten pregnant and was also very active in the church. They had gone on a camping trip with the Sunday school department when she met him. Gordon is his name. A strong, well-built hunk of a young man. Perfect body measurements. Even skin tone and a confidently handsome face. But there was nothing between the ears, according to Amy. "It seemed as if the gods must have given young Mister Gordon a head for one purpose and one purpose only." She had said. "And that purpose? Is to wear fine hats of all shapes, sizes, and colors." He added a much-enhanced flavor to youth camp that year, though. She was much too fascinated by him to notice the real Gordon in those early days it would have seemed. They started dating right away and very soon afterward. She fell for his magnetism and charms and got pregnant for him.

How surprised she was to become, at the number of folks, mainly church folks. Folks whose pieces of advice to her, mostly so-called "motherly advice," to her, was to abort it. Those were the hardest things for her to swallow. She understood it when it was coming from classmates and friends at school. But coming from the people in the church, her very own church? She never saw that one coming.

"I'm keeping my child," she declared quite firmly and forcefully. And that was just what she did. As for the young man, this Gordon chap. There, right there was where any and every hope he might have cherished of having a long-term relationship with Amy ended. "Thanks for my child," she told him. "And have a great life, you deserve it."

But it was not going to be with her. She was done with him, for good.

Sister Mills, as it turned out wasn't one who took very kindly and well to rejection. Right after she was done telling the congregation that Brother Gervis was checking her out. Brother Gervis got up from the keyboard. Picked up his coat and briefcase and walked right on out. With not even so much as a word of farewell, to anyone. Sister Mills got the message loud and clear, and she didn't take it very well. Whatever life she had left in her up until that point. Slowly seeped out of her, one day at a time. The strings that had been there holding her little heart together. Suddenly gave out one Sunday morning, while on route to church, in the car. Paramedics came by and picked her up from the car right there by the side of the road, dead. Although she had had health issues practically all her life. The general consensus from most of those people, including her church family - heck. Chiefly coming from her church family. The consensus was that she had died of a broken heart. Folks said that she had never been touched. Except for the fact that her life had certainly been touched by the hand of God. There was no denying that part. In the mortal, the human sense of the word, though. She was as unspoiled as they come. Depending on what angle one may be looking at it from. Some of us might be thinking the exact opposite: that she, in that regard, was as spoiled as they can get. As for me, and as for the doggy kind of man that I am. I do think that some things in this life are meant to be for a while. A very short while and not forever. And when those said "not-for-keeps" kind of things are kept unused for too long a time. They tend to get in everyone's way, even mine.

Fast-forward to a year later, and now, "Sister Amy and Brother Gervis" is a phrase that is dripping off everyone's tongue. As sweet and smooth as honey from the honeycomb. How quickly do we forget? Sister Mills had not settled in her graveclothes properly yet. But everyone has forgotten about Sister Mills and has moved on to the next in line for the fabulous prize of Doctor G. As in Gervis. Those other two, Brother Gervis and Sister Amy, had quickly closed the gap on the rest of the field and had become an item. His son Desmond and hers Zach, have managed to hit it off too. The friendship between Zach and Desmond is fast becoming legendary. In the meantime, pressure is building up in the church's inner circle. The "m" word just keeps on popping up in every conversation surrounding the newly arrived and crowned lovebirds. Yes, we're talking about the letter "m" here, as in marriage. At the same time, everyone seemed to be pinning their hopes and dreams on young Brother Ross. The bright and shining star prospect of a young preacher. Seemingly, without asking him first if that is in fact, what he wants for his life. Everybody has of late been referring to him not just as Brother Ross anymore, as was the custom. Now he has, seemingly, risen to the ranks of deacon and pastor in the eyes of many. Some have even been heard calling him "bishop." It's like he has already attained those heights in some people's minds. The poor chap, though, seemed to be on the verge of breaking under the weight of all of the expectations. Those expectations that they're piling up on his slender shoulders. But hardly anyone seemed to have noticed that part.

Meanwhile, he's getting older by the day. Not in ways as we all are, but the years are certainly showing themselves boldly upon young Bro. Ross. But none of the dream weavers and destiny shapers who're actively charting his course in life for him seem to have envisioned a life for him that included a wife, children, and a real career that included him earning his keeps. Such things haven't shown up anywhere in the mix, it would seem. In their scheme of earthly things for that young man. How misguided can some of us get to be sometimes, but what do I know? I may well be the most misguided person of them all. And there are certainly those who will be quick to suggest just that and will be showing up armed with evidence and facts to support those claims too. So, "Wait on who? Yes, the Lord," so they say, "Wait." To the young man, and "wait," is what he is doing. He is still waiting, right at this minute. Such a waste, such a pity. He has got a good heart, so polite and all. He would never even think of rebutting any of their claims and suggestions regarding him. Especially when those suggestions usually come to him in the name of the Lord. What can go wrong if it's the Lord's sayings and doings? You tell me.

Bro Gervis was taking his son Desmond back home to his mother in Vaudreuil-Dorion after having him spend the weekend with him in Montreal. This came about as part of shared parenting agreements. They had a fantastic time together, both of them. Both on the home front as well as elsewhere in the community. He has always tried to use the time he has with his son, to teach and show him some "man things." But this time, they also did quite a few other things, on the outside of the home kinds of man things, "many other such 'man things' too." Which was to be just as enjoyable for both of them. They went to the Bell Center to see the Montreal Canadians versus the Boston Bruins hockey game on Saturday night and then. Come Sunday morning, it was Brother Gervis and his son Desmond, all dressed up and in church, together. Fabulous, ain't it? His ex-wife doesn't feel the same way as he does about the church. Or even "the God thing." As she likes to put it. But, Gervis had argued that: "What he and his son do during their time together is for him and his son to decide. As long as Desmond is okay with it," he'd said, that is what they are going to be doing. As it turns out. Desmond doesn't mind going to church with his Papa. So church it was, both of them together there.

It was Sunday night and Desmond had got to be home with his mother in Vaudreuil-Dorion by nine. Ten o'clock at the latest. It was a good drive to get there. Nothing unusual, he was even ahead of time. They were discussing the events of the weekend in general and of the day's service in the church in particular when - out of nowhere. The SUV swerved around the truck. While trying to overtake a long line of vehicles. The rogue driver nipped the rear bumper of the car in front and to the left of their vehicle and shot right across the path of Gervis' car. Before he could even mount a timely response, the cars slammed into each other and flipped over, both of them. There, in St Anne de Bellevue on the westbound highway 40. A total of nine vehicles were involved in the pile-up there and were burning. Most of them. Burning there on the Trans-Canada highway. They didn't stand a chance. The authorities had to use the jaws of life to cut many of them out of the mangled wreck. Including the father and his son. Gervis and Desmond: Did they die before the fire consumed the car? No one was able to say for sure, not in our hearing, at least. Even up until the time of these writings. But they are, nonetheless, dead.

Amy went into mourning for an extended period. For the man, Gervis whom she had loved so very much and was preparing to marry. That was then, this is now.

Chapter Ten: Coming to a Town Near You.

The Millers wanted to do things to me, one wanted to grind. The other wanted to grind me up, like mincemeat.

It was in my teen years. I was about fifteen or sixteen at the time. I ran away from home and hitched a ride on a delivery truck into the big city of Toronto. Luckily for me, I'd managed to find myself a job that very day. A gardener and an errand boy with a rather wealthy family. I had arrived, I thought to myself.

The man, the master of the house, was a businessman. CEO of a nationwide manufacturing and distribution business outfit. The woman, though, as it turned out, was his wife, because. At first, I thought that she was probably his daughter or some other relative of his. Because of the obvious massive age difference between them. She seemed to me to be rather mean and sad at heart most of the time. But she also came across as awfully sweet at other times. I never did see any signs of children around the house. If there were any, I thought, they were probably living somewhere else. Then one day, it so happened that the mister man, Mr. Miller. Had to go overseas on some business trips. That was when it was to have happened.

She'd asked me to come inside and tend to the kitchen sink. "The wastewater outlet pipe," she said, was leaking and dripping water onto the kitchen floor. Why did I suddenly feel so uncomfortable? Why all of those knots in my stomach? Oh well! I consoled myself. It was probably nothing more than the fact that. I have never done anything even remotely resembling a plumbing job before. But I'm a fast learner, a willing hand, and a guy who really needed a job, this job.

She had all the tools on hand that were necessary to get the job done. On this particular day, it seems to me as if it was one of her better days. She seemed exceptionally exuberant. Spirited, helpful, and generous, and was rather perky in her overall mannerisms too. The problem was quickly spotted and just as quickly rectified. There was nothing wrong with the pipes more than a loose connecting coupling on the p-trap. In no time I was done with tightening it up. But she seemed to be searching all over the place for more and more chores for me to do. In the meantime, she wanted to know all that she could about me and the more I divulged, the more she dug in.

What started out as mere small talk quickly escalated to the point where I was even telling her all about the escapades between my fairy godmother and me. Perked her up really quick, and then, after she was done with getting me to bare my soul to her. My physical appearance was to be her next target. She began eyeing me from head to toe.

"Oh! I forgot," she said, "the one upstairs needed fixing too."

"What one upstairs?"

"The basin in the bathroom upstairs," she replied. "There's something wrong with the basin drainpipe up there, maybe you can take a look at it too since you're already here." So up the stairs, we went. She in the lead, and nervous, shaking in-my-boots, little old me, in-toe. She was talking very loudly as we mounted up the stairs. Maybe she was nervous but not nearly as nervous as I was. Her heavy army-like footsteps were pounding on the hardwood too. As she mounts upon them, mine, in contrast, was soft and well thought out.

"Mind you wake the baby up," I hear Bubbles saying in my inner ear.

"What baby you fool," said I, in my near-inner voice. Her perplexed gaze caught me off guard.

"What? What baby are you talking about now?"

"Never mind." I said, "I was just thinking out loud."

There were no repairs to be done up there. Well, no repairs, that is, unless. Unless we can categorize what was to have happened next as repairs... It probably was. In her lazy, heavy-tongued West African accent, she said, "So, you're Missa lover-man, eh? Lemme see what you have here, gimme some a-you best stuff."

"What about your husband?" I asked. "What if he should find out?"

"You don't have to worry bout he, or nothing else oh. I'll take good care ov-you, and him."

"I'm scared," I protested. "Suppose Mr. Miller should..."

"Eh! Eh!" she interrupted. "He's 93-year-old oh. What is he going to do? Eh, what is he going to do? Even if he should come inside here at this minute. What, is, he, going, to, do? To me. Or you?"

She was saying all that one word at a time while poking her index finger, with a sharp nail, hard on my forehead. As if to make sure that each letter. Each syllable, each word, was firmly registered somewhere in there. When she'd asked for my help to fix the sink drain. I'd obliged. When she'd asked me up the stairs to go and check out the bathroom plumbing. I also oblige. Well, she now finds it necessary to check out my best stuff and to show me hers. So what do you think I'm going to do? I reached into my ever-ready tool chest for my trusted nails and hammer and went to work nailing her to the ceramic tiles all over the bathroom floor. And up the steep climbing walls too. It felt like heaven's practice run to me. Will this be enough to set her straight? Set her straight maybe. Enough? Not on your life.

For the remainder of the two and a half years while I was "working" there. We made it a point of our duty to paint the entire house. From the attic to the bloody-bleeding basement. The mister man was fast closing in on us. Getting much too close to clamp down on us. Well, (on me in particular,) much too close for my comfort. That was when I'd packed up my little trinket box and kitty bags and skipped the scene. I went back home to my mother's place, and then back to school to study computer science. Mrs. Miller was not as willing and ready as I was to move on. Not at all. She would seek me out at every opportune time to get her welding done. When I got engaged to Aylene, she wished me well. She wished us both well. Of course, she couldn't do that on the phone. She needed to come to see me in person. That was the last time we were together in any one place again. By our lonesome selves. Of course, nothing happened then. Nothing more has ever happened between us since either. Not even so much as a single, solitary, wayward phone call.

Chapter Eleven: Hearing, Seeing, Smelling, Tasting.

We picked up our partially eaten meals and briskly walked out of the diner. I grabbed hold of a few extra sheets of paper towels on the way out. "We might need them to clean up," I said, should in case we happen to spill any of the gravy from the silicone cup. The creamy, tasty poutine was beginning to get a bit cold and soggy in the sauce. But that didn't take away from my cravings for it. What had caused us to ditch the joint so hurriedly was the alarmingly loud smell emanating from the girl. The one who had just come in and sat down at the table in the farthest (but not quite far enough for my liking,) corner from us. The smell was unbearable.

"Wow! Can you believe that?" I said while we were exiting the building. "Has she not yet heard of something called deodorant?"

"Or just plain old soap and water," Libby added. "Maybe she doesn't realize that she smelled though," she pounced in the girl's defense.

"Come on!" I countered. "How could she not know that? She's as loud as a bullhorn at the county fair."

"To us, she may be as loud as a bullhorn at the county fair but to her. It may not be so pronounced."

"What are you saying?"

"Have you ever gone into a restroom? And have to beat a hasty retreat when the smell from inside hits you? Or let me put it another way. Have you ever used the restroom yourself, and just as soon as you were done and walked out, you turned around to see someone else walking in and had to beat a swift escape when the odor you'd left behind you, hit them square in the face?"

"Please, don't spoil my appetite. That's not the type of thing I want to be talking about over my lunch."

"Oh, come on Mister "Chicken-chest." Well, if you think that's too gross for your lunch-hour conversation. Let's try another analogy here. Okay, let's say it's garlic breath then. How many people are ever aware that they have that before others start resenting them? Or until someone who's kind and caring points it out to them?"

"So, what exactly are you saying here?"

"I just think that we might have gone about it the wrong way."

"And what is the right way as you see it - Miss Lib?"

"Lib? Where did that one come from?"

"Off my tongue, it just rolled that easily off my tongue, why?"

"It's just that no one else has ever called me that except."

"Yes? Except whom?"

"Never mind that, let's get back to the point at hand."

"No, I want to hear this, except who?"

"My mother, she always calls me that. Are you satisfied?" ugh! "Maybe we should have told her", she continued.

"Are you crazy? You mean you want us to walk up to her, to this total stranger, and say: hey, you stink?"

"No, that's not what I'm saying. Not like that, not in those words. Or even in that tone. Put yourself in her shoes for a moment here. If everybody just keeps on running away from you, beating a swift escape every time they get anywhere near you. Not taking the time to talk to you, (nicely). And to tell you what the problem is, you might never know. Taking the garlic analogy into consideration here."

"So you mean, you want to become her angel of mercy? You want to go save her from the demon she likely doesn't even know that she has?"

"Not really, but everyone does need a friend sometimes. And maybe we could become friends with her. Befriend her and guide her into something better than that."

"I don't want to be any sort of friends with someone like that."

"Like what? She's a human being. A living, breathing person with a beating heart, with feelings like you and me."

"Why can't her own folks teach and guide her? Why has it got to be left up to others to do it? Why me, or you?"

"Maybe she's got no one here, she could be here in this city all by herself you know. Just like many of the people whom we pass on the street. Or sit beside when on the bus, or even those whom we may run into in the classrooms daily. She might just need guidance. She might just need a friend."

"What if we just give her some deodorant? You know, what if we could just stick it somewhere where she's bound to find it? She'll get the message, don't you think?"

"No, no, you don't do things like that to people. That would be even worse than if we just left her alone and let her be. And that's what everyone seems to be doing already as it is. And that's not helping her any - right?"

"So, can we just get back to doing just that: leave her alone and let her figure it out for herself? And let's just eat what's left of our meal?"

By this point, we were sitting in the car, and I was starting to feel a bit cold and chilly, so I fired up the car engine, turned the heat on, and up to the full blast. We still had lots of time on our hands. And neither one of us wanted to split and leave each other's company. Well, so it would have seemed to me, not quite yet. So, I exited the parking spot just before the zeros started flashing indicating the expiration of the toll.

"Where are you going?" She asked.

"Somewhere nice and adorable, you'll see."

"Tell me, tell me, I don't like surprises."

"You'll love this one, I promise." I took de Maisonneuve Boulevard and navigated over to rue Guy. I then headed up Cote des Neige Road and over the mountain. You know where I was headed, don't you? Got to go see old St Joseph on top of the hill.

Libby was thrilled with the view. She was just standing there looking down on that section of Montreal. West of the hill. I had to drag her away. "Come on, there's much more for you to see." We went inside and did a tour of several of the points of interest. We were even in time to catch the day's communion service in the cathedral, or at least one of them since they probably do several of those each day. I'm still not quite sure about that one though. But we sat in on it. We were trying to be as reverent and attentive as we possibly could. Yes, we took the sacrament and the cup too. Everybody there seemingly did. The smell of all those burning candles was the next thing to hit us from the elevator. We followed our noses as well as the moving crowd into the "room of the millions of burning candles." That's what we were to have named it on the spot. I managed to convince her to light a candle and say a prayer at the shrine of Brother Andre. I whispered a small prayer to myself too.

"What did you pray for?" Bubbles wanted to know.

"My business and mine only," said I, "thank you very much."

On the way out I dropped a coin in the big pot, (that's what I call it.) and tossed a penny into the makeshift wishing well too. Libby followed suit... It would appear as if it was all those rituals. Or at least some of them that were having somewhat of a positive, calming effect on us. Both of us. Or was it the spirit? Could have been, you know? We were feeling refreshed and much lighter as we exited the building and the compound as a whole.

"I really enjoyed it," she said while we were walking across the parking lot towards the car. "So, I guess you were right," she continued.

"Right about what?"

"You did say that I would enjoy it and I did."

"Well," I said, "we're not quite done yet, we've got one more sight to go and see."

"What is it? What is it?"

"You'll see when we get there."

I drove back over the mountain to the lookout point on the other side and stopped. Again, she was charmed by the view. We were looking over to the other side of the city of Montreal East and north-eastward and aided this time with the magnetic lens.

"Can you believe this?" Libby chirped. "That I was born and raised right here in this city and it's the first time I'm seeing this?"

As for me? I could believe it alright. It was quite easy for me to believe. Her life, alongside that of her entire family, seemed to me to exist in a bubble. Where the only thing that matters to them is work, work, and more work. And money, money, money. They never seem to take a moment to just live a little and breathe. I think all of that is about to change for Libby now though, well, I hope so.

When her phone rang, it was Kamal, her brother. Called to say that he was on his way to get her. We've got to get back down to Sherbrooke Street and McGill College soon. Preferably before he gets there. So, we hopped into the car and headed down the winding road off Mount Royal to get back to McGill.

Kamal was there alright, waiting. He was waiting there in the car when we got there. I turned off Sherbrooke and onto Union Street then onto President Kennedy and dropped Libby off on the corner of President Kennedy and University streets. She then walked from there to get to where Kamal was parked on Sherbrooke Street. Was waiting for her. She said she just wasn't in the mood for an argument or to be answering a barrage of questions. And that was why she had asked me to drop her off on the corner and out of sight of her brother. She leaned across the seat and gave me a kiss on the cheek before turning to leave. I grabbed hold of her arm and pulled her back towards me. Then leaned in and kissed her. And then kiss her again, yes, on the lips.

I've gotta go, she said, before exiting the vehicle and briskly walking away.

Bye, Lib.

Bye.

Chapter Twelve: The Stakeout.

Several days had now passed without us seeing each other, that's Libby and me. The hunger built up within me and burns hot. I knew I had to go back and try to see her. But how could I go without an invitation? Oh well! I knew just the right thing to do - I had a plan.

"I'll go and stake her out. Stake out the points where I knew that she frequents. Where she's most likely to be seen, where she's most likely to walk on by while I'm sitting there."

I sat in my car, just a block away from the diner. One stoplight away in a far direction from where she usually makes the approach. The park is just across the street from the diner. So, whether she chooses to have her meal there in the diner or over in the park. Either place will be right smack in front of my eyeballs. I wasn't there more than a minute before she showed up. And both venues were good just as I had thought.

She came walking briskly and purposefully through the park. Walked across the street and headed straight into the diner. I moved the car up a bit closer. Just passed over the intersection and stopped. I then sat in the car with the motor running and watched through the rolled-up tinted window. She was at the back of a line of five or six other people. Her arms folded across her breasts. She was looking over her shoulders periodically as if she was expecting to see someone.

Bubbles: "Could it be that she's looking for you - Buddy?"

"Butt out, will you?" I rebuked him. She looked over this shoulder and then that, and at one point. I'm sure I saw her looking at the table where we had sat when we were both inside there sometime before. And that was more than just a lingering glance. For some unknown reason, at that point, I felt a rush of warmth deep down in my belly. I pulled out of the space and went searching for a proper parking spot. Parked the car and fed enough money for an extra half hour into the parking meter, and then. Walked briskly back towards the diner. She saw me on the approach and turned full faced towards me with her still folded arms across her chest as she waited. With a sneaky look and a thin smile plastered on her face.

"Hi, Libby."

"Hello, Mr. Woodhardt." She greeted me with a homie, long-time-pal sort of a hug. Harbinger of things to come, perhaps. Hmm

Bubbles: "Wow, what did you do for that one?"

Libby: "What's up with you, where, have, you, been?" those words came dropping in on the front of my shirt.

Me: "Around, been busy. How have you been doing yourself, are you okay?"

"Hmm-um," she nodded and shook her head. "Just was a bit concerned about you when I did not see you in these last few days." I was just about to say: why didn't you call me? But just then I was to have recollected that we hadn't gotten that far as yet, not so far as to have exchanged numbers. And with those people still there around us who'd just witnessed the warm familiar type of embrace we'd just engaged in. I didn't want to spoil it and leave them all in puzzlement as to what was really going on.

Libby: "I was just about to grab something to eat. Should I order for both of us? Pizza as usual I suppose?"

"I'm good with that, you know me just a little too well." We laughed.

We sat down at the table. Just like we did on the very first occasion there. The only difference this time was that she didn't have a pile of books in front of her. However, she seemed just as focused and purposeful as ever. Was she focused on the task of getting to know me? I mean, to really know me this time. "I'd hope so."

"So, what have you been doing?" She asked me again.

"As I have said, I've been busy with work and studies. Work, more so than studies. Did I not tell you about the gig I had to go and do at the techno center last evening? Thought I did."

"Yes, you did mention it, but I didn't know it would be taking you that long."

Bubbles: "that long? She misses you - dude..."

"So what happened at the Techno Center? Did you say that something occurred there that...?"

"I don't want to talk about it," I interrupted her. I didn't think that we were at that place yet. I wasn't sure how she would view the whole thing. Would she think that I had something to do with it? In leading the woman on? Thinking that I was flirting with her or something? I didn't want her to see me like that. But then again. Would that view of me as seen through her eyes, like, of who I was? Or of how I would behave in such events, in her mind! Would that be a misrepresentation of the facts? Maybe my fame had gone on ahead of me and had featured prominently in the Madam's decision to hire me. In which case, I couldn't deny the accuracy of her assessment of the whole mess. But for once in my life, I didn't want this person, this woman with the heavenly glow and vivacious energy to see me in that light. It had suddenly dawned on me that this one, for some strange reason, mattered to me, a lot.

My mother used to say in the old days: that only the vain and clueless man is led to believe that his whole life's purpose and vocation is to make his woman happy. "There's much more to life than that," she had said, but. Since meeting up with this woman, Libby Dahoust, I'm not sure anymore man, I'm just not sure. But I'm willing to go out of my way to at least try to make this one woman happy. If not to piss my mother off. Then, maybe it's to get a chance to see where things lead from here. With Libby and I. Not quite sure where Mom stands in this regard when it comes to Amy and other female folks. She would probably say the very same thing, with just a bit of alteration of the gender parts of those sayings to make them fit. But as for Norm and me? She never fails to remind us of this, her version of what the truth in the facts of life is or is supposed to be.

Chapter Thirteen: Exes, O's and Horse Riders.

On my birthday. I was to get the most unexpected, sweetest voice-mail ever. Followed by a follow-up call later that evening. From whom did you ask? None other than my beloved ex-wife. What was she up to this time, hmm? When it rains, it pours.

"Just called to wish you a happy birthday dear," she said. But it was obvious that that was not all that she wanted to talk about.

"Maybe we should have tried a little bit harder to make our marriage work when we had it." She went on to say. "Maybe it was not all that bad after all. Maybe we could take another kick at the can," can we? She asked further.

An awful lot of maybe, maybe, maybe. Ain't it?

"It's a bit late for that now don't you think?"

"Well, we all have made our mistakes, nobody's perfect. But mistakes can be corrected, can't they? What can one do with perfection?"

"Not much," I replied sarcastically. "How is your husband doing these days?" I then asked, emphasizing the "husband." Silence, "uh uh! Just as I thought." I said before ending the call.

...

Dan Ryder was the champion jockey that year. He was vying for a second straight year in the enviable position. But then came the big fall. He was riding the big mount: Run-for-joe, who was vying to become the horse of the year too. They were in slot number three of seven in the Gold Cup race.

Run-for-joe was no doubt the two-to-one favorite. But strong challenges were expected from the likes of Rude Boy and Jeremy's Pet. Dan Ryder's friend and competition jockey-Wayne Martin wasn't riding in the race. And since he himself was not in the running for any big prizes, like, trophies, or top honors that time around. There was no doubt that all his support was behind his friend-Danny.

The stands were jam-packed with race-watchers and spectators of all stripes and colors. As the horses burst out of the starting gates. Run-for-Joe broke nicely and quickly staked out her favorite position to the far left of the field. Miracles and wonders then broke out into the lead ahead of Jeremy's Pet, and Holiday-Season. Followed closely by Rude Boy, Simplicity, and March Break bringing up the rear. As they approach the halfway mark. Run-for-Joe was in the lead, but Rude Boy began to find his footing and pounced ahead of the rest of the field to sit in the second position. Jeremy's Pet was sitting in the catbird seat at third. Poised and ready to bounce back at any moment.

The race was between those three. Meanwhile, March break, surprisingly though it seemed to many, was putting on a gallant challenge up the middle. As the finish line approached, it was Rude Boy, Jeremy's Pet, and Run-for-Joe. Coming down to the wire. It's Rude boy and Run-for-joe, Rude boy, Run-for-joe. Run-for-Joe just knocked Rude Boy right over the finish line for a photo-finish win.

But that was not all that was to have happened there and then. It would have appeared as if the last-minute push to the finish line by Run-for-Joe was just a bit too much on the horse's legs and caused her left front leg to snap and break at the joint just above the horseshoe. The animal stumbled and fell right through the finish line to secure the win for her owners and supporters, but as for the horse herself, she did not fare quite as well. The horse's leg wasn't the only thing broken there that day. The fall was much too powerful on the animal's neck which hit the ground first. They had to put the poor beast down. Some folks I know, though, thought that they should have put the injured jockey down too. Right there and then.

The jockey was carried away on a stretcher with a broken left leg and a fractured hip. Never mount up on a horse again. At least not in a professional capacity. I've got a funny feeling that he has been having trouble mounting up on some other beastly things too. Other than the feline kind. Based on the evidence that has been showing up of late, even on the phone line. His beloved wife, out of the blue, remembered my phone number and took to calling me up. She'd called me on my birthday to wish me a happy birthday.

I've been doing quite well in the (happy) department of my life of late, I told her. When I needed your wishes, your thoughts, and your actions for my happiness. It was never forthcoming. On the contrary, you went out of your way at every juncture to ensure that the opposite was true for me. But that was then, I said, this is now. She sure seems to be putting in some extra time on the task of working her way back to me, with a burning love inside of late. One can always hope, I suppose. Can't they?

...

One will always need to be spell-specific when referring to him and when calling or writing his name in order to separate who Dan Ryder is, from what he does. Whenever they call him by his name: Ryder. One is never quite sure if it's Ryder, the name he'd inherited from his father, or if it's "Rider" the jockey.

They were buddies from school days. That's Wayne Martin and him. When Wayne Martin quit Secondary School and went on to sign up for jockey school. His friend Dan Ryder wasn't far behind. I ended up dating his sister. We were married not long afterward. We were both young and still very much in love. We were both in college at the time too. And our parents agreed that we could share living facilities. Alternating between her mother's place and mine. My mother had given me the basement at home. I eventually got it fixed up and made it as comfortable as I could. It wasn't the Ritz Carlton. But it was our home and we were in love, or so I thought. Everything seemed set for us to take off and flourish. But then, those two started showing up more and more frequently and were busily showering everyone with gifts and goodies. She wanted that type of lifestyle for herself. Easy access to cash and kinds too, I guess. And I couldn't afford to give it to her, yet. But I kept on reminding her that our future was looking good. "Things will get better soon," I told her constantly but... She was in the "now" frame of mind. The future was way too far away for her. Discontent set in next and then came the blame and the complaints.

At 29 I was still living in the basement apartment at my mother's place. Because I could not afford the rent and bills that accompanied an independent lifestyle. I even ended up having to sell my car at one point. Because I couldn't afford the fuel, upkeep, and maintenance. And then, I committed a faux pas that turned out to be the blamed catalyst for the final breakup of my marriage. I'd picked up a gift for her at one of the pawnshops that I used to frequent, a bad gift it was. Don't ask what it was though, can't tell you that. I then started out on a search for better. Was to find my calling in the world of the computer. All things to do with computers. Among a few other things, yes. She moved out of my place back to her mom's place. "Just wanted to be alone for a while to figure things out," she'd said. She never came back. The divorce was easy. She wanted it so I let her have it. Didn't stand in her way. And we didn't have anything to split up since we didn't have anything, yet.

...

Two years into the marriage. I had started working the night shift -you know? The real dark, wild side type of night shift. Taking a walk on the darker side of the street, one might say.

It was the culmination of a number of things that had brought it about. I'd just gotten sick and tired of depending on my mother to bail me out financially. The wife was upping the ante. Becoming more and more discontented. I couldn't just sit there and twiddle my thumb. I had to do something. So, I got a brand-new toolkit and went to work. From car theft to home invasion. Whatever gets me the bacon to take back home. That's what I'd do. The pawnshops around town all knew my face. I was a regular in and out of those joints. On both ends of the deal too. When I was not selling, I was buying. It was at one of those places that I'd picked up a gift for her (the wife) on her birthday. A very inappropriate gift for a birthday present from a loving husband to his wife, one might say. But then again, what can a poor boy do? Not enough, obviously. That was when she moved out of my place. And went back into her mom's place. "For a while," she'd said. As it was to turn out? It was a very short "while." She did call me up again though, at least one more time.

Out of the blue, she called. The raindrops were pitter-pattering on the windowsills. What calming effects it had on me. It gets to me every single time. It could as well rain every day for me for all I cared. If it was only for this (and yes, a few other reasons.) But then came the interruption.

"Hello," I answered the ringing telephone.

"What are you doing?" She asked.

"I'm planting tulips."

"Planting tulips? In this weather?"

"Yes, it's the best weather, the best time and season for that-didn't you know?"

"For planting tulips?"

"Yes, for planting tulips. As in, not one, but two-lips."

She hung up. Never did call back.

I couldn't suppress the laughter. No matter how hard I was to have tried.

It was raining there too, I was sure. Right there where she was. And it was obviously having those sorts of effects on her mood. Yes, those. She needed some company, the right kind of company. That was why she'd called me up. Sorry, Missy, those days are long gone.

Chapter Fourteen: Me and Mrs. B?

I still have some unfinished business with Ms. Brodbendt that needs some tending to.

On the Walk to the bus stop. I was singing away: "I shot the sheriff, but I did not shoot..."

"What?" Bubbles butted in, and he wanted to know. "You did not shoot what? Ms. Brodbendt's furry old pussycat? You probably should have," he said.

Cute, very cute.

...

After that close encounter of the worst kind with me thinking that I was going to get lucky and hit the jackpot playing poker with Ms. B., it never worked out as I had planned. Did in fact hit something. But it wasn't the jackpot. At least not the one that I'd placed a bet on. Nor was it in the way I wanted it to be. But there's always another day, and one can always dream I suppose.

Didn't have to wait very long. The following afternoon I was called to the principal's office, again. For the first time in a long time though. I was feeling rather apprehensive about going into Ms. Brodbendt's office. It was like I'd done something really bad, only worse. I couldn't remember ever feeling so bad going in there. Even if it was after getting into some kind of trouble but, on this day. I was so very nervous that even the locks of hair on my head seemed to be sweating. Guess I was a bit ashamed of myself for... for whatever reason. Letting down Ms. B perhaps? Or, letting myself down in Ms. B's presence? Me not living up to expectations. Not measuring up to the billing? Ms. B's mission on this day, it would seem, was to reassure me. To smooth over the bruised ego for me. She was so sweet and understanding, in the way she spoke to me.

"Don't you go beating up on yourself," she told me this when she was to further say: "You're perfectly okay, nothing is wrong with you, nothing at all. As a matter of fact, I think it was rather sweet." She winked at me and smiled.

"What do you say? You can come over again this afternoon, and I'll show you how to do it right?" I didn't respond. Just sat there staring at the boots on my shaking feet on the floor, but then, to the house, we went. Ms. Brodbendt and I.

"Yay..." I stifled a shout. "Ms. Brodbendt and me?" I said, when I... "We're taking it all the way home-baby." I was sure that Bubbles heard me. But he never said a word in response.

...

"Go have a shower." Ms. Brodbendt commanded me as soon as we got home to her house. I was more than a bit self-conscious and resented the way that came across. Is she saying that I stink? I tucked my nose under my armpits as soon as she turned her back. Can't say that it was scentless or pleasant. But still, come on, give a guy a break here. Won't you?

However, whenever Ms. Brodbendt says jump. I usually ask, how high? So I went to the bathroom and got my shower. Just like she wanted. Must admit though. I felt a whole lot better afterward. Now it's her turn, to get a shower. I sat on the couch and grabbed the remote control for the TV. Turn the big box on and flick through channel after channel. Just to kill some time. Trying to pacify the nervous tensions within.

I didn't hear the shower going like it was going the last time. Instead, the bathtub was filling up. I could hear the water running out of the faucet and into the tub. Ms. Brodbendt called out to me from inside the bathroom. "Manley! Come here, Manley." I didn't budge, "Manley!" She called out again, after the third time. I slowly got up and walked up to the door. And even more slowly I turned the doorknob and pushed it open. She was in the bathtub, covered up with mushy white bubbles. I edged my way back out through the open door, in the same way as I came in, before.

"Come here," she said in a sort of whiny high-pitched whisper while stretching out her right hand over and across the edge of the bathtub. Reeling me in with those calling fingers of hers.

"No." I said, "I don't want to. I don't feel too good."

I pulled the door closed while walking back out. I wasn't sure why, but I did feel somewhat restrained from just gabbling up Miss B. like that. It probably was because of the office. Her station in life, her role in my life. "She's the principal...," I whispered to myself, "for crying out loud."

I didn't feel quite the same way about doing things to get my fairy godmother's mojo going. Even though they were both similar to each other in many ways. Both of them were teachers, roughly the same age. Same physical make-up, appearance, and body types, but still. If it was Gaddy's, my fairy godmother's place that I had gone to like that. The TV would still be as cold as icicles. Since I'd not be turning it on. I'd be busy right off the cuffs, getting the biggest bang for my hard-earned bucks. Working the late shift and overtime too, working on my fairy godmother's bus. And also on the brand-new second-hand Volvo, parked over there by us. The only thing that would be needing to get a turn-on after we get inside the house and close the door behind us. It would have been me taking out the jackhammer keys and turning it over to Gaddy. Since both of us would have had our other hard and even the soft metallic mechanism and auto body parts already turned on and heated up to a fever pitch. Even before we'd managed to bust in through the half-opened door, like this. But as for Ms. B? It's going to take a lot more out of me. Getting used to the idea that I could bang on her door in a similar manner. And to think that I really, really wanted so very much to be doing just that. More than anything in the world at this stage of my life, my teenage boy's life.

She came through the door and stood in the passageway. With nothing but a big bath towel wrapped around her, like, this way. I saw this from the corner of my eye since I wasn't looking directly at her. She came over to me where I was sitting on the couch. Took me by the hand and led me into the bedroom and into the big queen size bed and into...

"What? You mean you want me to tell you every little bit of the gory details, just like that?" She'd made me promise not to tell, you know? Those were the conditions under which we had gotten that far.

Suffice it to say, though. Not only did the innocence and inhibitions tumble and fall there that evening, but the oversized, wrap-up-my-sexy-mama bath towel came crashing down to the floor too.

Chapter Fifteen: How Do You Spell Relief Again?

She was almost done with the exams and done with swatting the studies. She accepted my invitation to go out somewhere else. Somewhere other than the usual little diner across the street where we used to go to eat. She wanted us to go see a movie.

"What are you going to do about your brother? Your chauffeur, whenever he gets back here to pick you up? And also, for the rest of your family when you get back home, and they start quizzing you as to your whereabouts?" I'd asked this because she never seems to go anywhere or do anything without their blessings, and their participation too, to some extent.

"I'm a grown woman," was her response, "haven't you noticed?"

"Oh yeah, I notice. And what a relief it is to hear you say that. Speaking of relief, how do you spell relief again?"

"R-E-L-I-E-F? You mean you really didn't know?" "No, that's not it. It's spelled G-R-A-D-U-A-T-I-O-N." Ugh! She gasped and stared at me.

"You're so damn silly," she said.

I rested my case there and then and put it to bed.

Although it was not summering yet. And although it was a little bit on the nippy side, the weather that is. She was wearing a dress and heels, she was stunning. I couldn't keep my sneaky peaky eyes off her. Her long, beautiful legs were there. Just begging for attention, my attention, and care. I'd seen a bit of her lower legs before. Last summer I think it was when she wore a pair of shorts for a time, or two, to one of our meetups. But that was just slightly above the knee since she never wore them higher than that like the other girls usually do. We chatted about many things on the drive to the cinema. Or as far as we had managed to get on the route there before the trouble was to get started. She was highly confident that the exam results would be phenomenal. She had already gotten herself many jobs and offers coming her way from many and varied places.

Places such as Toronto, Ottawa, Victoria, and Vancouver. Even got at least three from cities in the US. Of course, Montreal's medical institutions were not to be left out of the bidding. Three hospitals in Montreal and other health facilities and clinics were bidding too.

Her father, and her mother to a lesser extent, were trying to get her to choose the Jewish General Hospital right here in Montreal. But she would rather not. She'd said that she wanted to get as far away from Montreal as possible. But I think it's not so much Montreal itself that she'd wanted to get away from but rather. Far away from me? Maybe. Or away from her overbearing parents. Though not as far away as some of us would like, she's leaning towards Ottawa, or Toronto, in that order. She said she likes those cities. And being as realistic a person as she is. It's just a two-hour drive back from Ottawa to Montreal for those occasional visits with her family and vice versa. Which is bound to happen.

"And we could link up from time to time too" I'd said. "Whenever you're in town, you and I, you know?"

"I was kind of hoping…"

"Hoping what?"

"Nothing."

"Hoping that I would join you on the move-right?"

"No, never mind me."

"That's exactly what you were about to say. I'll bet my lunch on it."

"You're getting a little bit too full of it-mister. That's not it at all."

"Too full of what?"

"Yourself, too full of your damn self. Like, like, you seem to think that you are God's gift to the world or something."

"I never said that at all, I only challenge you to finish the statement. Finish saying what you were about to say. And you can't, because, you know I'm right. But I can finish it for you. You were hoping that I would come along with you."

"Are you listening to yourself? Really? Talk about pompous."

"That's not being pompous. That's called being on point Missy.

And funny though it may seem, I was thinking the same damned thing too." Pause...

"What same thing are you talking about?"

"You know full well what I'm saying. And the answer is yes. I would love to."

Chapter Sixteen: Poetic Justice.

Mr. Personality got his car towed because. In his selfish desire to park. He blocked the whole road. And then the fines he was forced to pay amounted to quite a mighty load. Poetic justice lends itself well to the judicial code. While these cheering voices gave way to relieving breath from the nodding crowd

It was two days after the big snowstorm. Usable parts of most of the roadway were being reduced to about a third of the usual norm. The snow was piled up high at several points where the snowplows had pushed it. As I was inching my way along in the slow-moving traffic, trying to get out of the city. Libby was sitting right there beside me, seemingly oblivious to the time slowly slipping away.

We were finally nearing the end of the one-way street. After almost half an hour of just crawling through at the speed of a profane turtle en route to Sunday school. On lesson-review morning. This car was the one that was immediately in front of our car. Pulled off of the roadways. Venturing to breach the accumulating snow and slush to the left side of us in order to park.

Meanwhile, to the right of where he ended up parked was another stopped vehicle. Which seemed to us to be throttling. A man was sitting in the driver's seat, and chatting away on the phone. So, this second vehicle, braze the snow and slush and then stopped, crookedly. The driver shut down the engine and cracked the door open to get out. I tapped on the horn to solicit his attention. He turned and looked at me. Then quickly seemed to survey the long line of traffic behind me and then close the door to the driver's seat, (thud). And then proceeded to get a small boy out of the back seat. To go off somewhere I'd assumed. Again, I tapped on the horn very gently and rolled the window down. I stuck my head out the window and said, "Can you just move over a bit more so that the rest of us can pass by you?"

"Too much snow," he said. As he closed that door too (thud), the one out of which he had just taken the little boy and turned to walk away.

"So," I said. "Because there is 'too much snow' that makes it okay for you to block the entire street. And hinder everybody else from moving along?"

"Calm down," he said, "Calm down," and again he said, "Calm down." I was as calm as could be. And believe me, when I say, I was calm.

The snow of which we speak, (both him and I,) were of the slushy type. It tends to shift and move under the weight of the vehicles.

"He said to calm down," said Libby. "But he's the one who is aggressive here, passively aggressive."

He left this long line of vehicles stuck behind his crookedly parked street-blocking vehicle. Turned his head around while leaving and pointed in the other guy's direction to say: "Ask the other guy to move."

"He was there before you, I said. And neither of us, neither you nor I know if his vehicle is, in fact, mobile. But I'm sure your vehicle is."

"Yes," said Libby, "it's always the other person's responsibility to act, never yours or mine."

"Why am I even here arguing with you though?" He said as he took the child's hand and walked away, leaving everyone there stuck in grid-lock. Since I was sitting in my warm and comfortable car. Having my favorite person in the world (at this point in time.) Sitting right there next to me, and who seemed just as content with the thought of being here with me as she would being in the cinema staring at the screen, maybe even more so, I'd hoped.

I pulled off the roadway, parked behind his vehicle, and sat there. Just watching the scene... The driver of the pick-up truck that was immediately behind me wasn't as patient as the rest of us were. As soon as I'd pulled off and parked behind the agitator's vehicle. Navigating over much more of the very same sort of snow and slush that he was avoiding at every cost. The pick-up truck guy squeezed his way past my vehicle and proceeded to take the mirror off the crooked-parked vehicle while also leaving a long streak mark on the side of the vehicle for him to deal with when he got back. Did you all hear those shouts and cheers just now? It came from the many other satisfied drivers and onlookers who saw it as it went down, and whose faith has now been restored in the concept of Poetic Justice.

The very next vehicle that happened to pull up, though, was a city bus, whoa, whoa. Such a letdown, the people's bubbles had just been burst. If he, the bus driver, if he had followed the lead of the pick-up truck and just pushed that car out of the way. Man, oh, man! No matter what they were showing up at the cinema at that moment. It couldn't have rivaled the satisfaction that all of us looking on would have gotten out of it. But the bus driver was cut from a different cloth than the guy just before him. Or it could be just the fact that he, the bus driver. Has got a lot more responsibilities riding on him and his shoulder. He just stopped there, with his hazard lights going. Case closed, street closed, everything around these parts closed. There's a complete standstill now for traffic on this street. As if it wasn't so before. Next, there were flashing lights and sirens coming. The police car pulled up from the other direction and against the traffic flow and stopped. Then came the tow truck with yet more flashing lights. The wrecker proceeded to back up in front of the car. The crookedly parked car. Libby and I were not yet at the cinema. And at this rate, we probably won't make it there any time soon, but we're having the time of our lives. Showtime that is.

By now, look, the cop is coming out with his ticketing pad. The tow truck guy is moving into position too. And now… Here he comes, here he comes… Guess who? Yep. To the loudest applause ever. Entered the man of the hour, but. Hey! Why aren't you smiling, aren't you happy? You're the star of the show here, no? So now it's negotiating time. But neither the cop nor the tow truck guy was budging. So, the begging and pleading were to continue on until…

Not sure how it all went down with him thereafter. The good police officer and the tow guy did manage to clear the street enough to get us moving again and out of there.

Change of plans now for Libby and me. We had obviously lost so much time there that we would be late for the flick at the Guzzo cinema.

Quickly, very quickly, I thought of something else.

"Let's go to the outdoor cinema complex," I said. "Where is that?" She wanted to know.

"Where else? At Laval, of course. At the flea market site in Laval."

"Can you believe that guy though?" Libby commented when we hit the highway. "Some people are just so damn selfish. As long as he is at a place where he can park and get out. Or more so than that, it might have been exactly where he was going, to begin with. Everybody else could just drop dead, for all he cared."

"I bet he's starting to care a lot more by now," I argued. "About the money he'll have to pay for the ticket as well as for the towing if nothing else."

We were late for the early show. So, we went about killing some more time in the flea market. Just walking around, eye-shopping. And then we went and grabbed something to eat at a restaurant next door.

It was something somewhat different than what we have been having at the diners and pizzerias in Montreal. Pork and beans with maple sauce and hot home-style biscuits among other things it was. "A specialty of the region," we were told. We still had half an hour to spare after all of that, before the start of the show. So, we went back to the flea market. Just to browse around. Libby picked up an oil painting from one of the stalls there. A tiny little thing in the scheme of those things. It was just about four inches by six inches in diameter, but it was a real oil painting. It even had a signature on it. Unrecognizable to me, to either one of us. But a signature it was anyway, so.

I paid the twenty-five dollars the lady was asking for it. Over Libby's many protests and gave it to her.

"It might come to be worth something one of these days," I told her. "If not in monetary terms, at least in memory... Of your first outdoor cinema flick with somebody, like me." She giggled with glee as she tucked it away under her purse.

It was a bonanza of a movie deal for Libby and me. It was her first time ever going to an outdoor cinema. Where we just sit in the car and watch the movie on the big screen. But they were also showing one of my very favorite old movies: Magnificent Seven, "Yeah..." I said, "We're going back baby, way back."

"Note from the author." Just a note of thank you to you, my friend, for choosing to read my book and sticking with the story thus far. If you make it this far, I think it's a sign that you are enjoying the story. I want to ask you here, my reader, to take a minute or two to post a review of the book on the Sales Pages at Amazon. or any other such page. And don't keep it all to yourself, share it. This small gesture is so very important and very much appreciated. Thank you ever so much. Now, continuing on with the story

Chapter Seventeen: Problem? What Problem?

After the movie, I took her home. That was when and where the troubles were to get started...

Her parents were waiting for her, and when I say "waiting," I mean, they were literally standing there at the door kind of waiting. Yes, that's the kind of "waiting," for her.

"Who is this?" The father was to have asked even before any exchange of greetings, "Who is this?"

"Hi Dad, this is my friend Manley..."

"Manley, Manley who... What's this about?"

"As I said - Dad, he's a friend of mine. We go to the same school. He offered to take me home today and I accepted the offer. I never thought that that would pose a problem."

"Problem? Problem? Why would it be a problem? Let him in, come in, come on in, and tell us more. I want to hear some more about this..."

As of late. I've been finding myself playing a song over and over in my head and singing along to the lingering refrain. And it goes something like this:

"Miss Luba's one daughter, she's a girl I love. I'm going to marry her soon, under a silvery moon."

However, only bubbles and I would have known about me singing this little song. I was looking forward to popping the big question but not before consulting with them and receiving the blessings of the Dahoust family, of course. But after this encounter, after what was to have happened here on this night, I've got to be thinking of another song to sing:

"I'm not sure anymore, more.

Who's knocking at my door, door..."

Libby's family home is a duplex in Kirkland near the strip mall on St Charles Boulevard. All four of them used to occupy the main floor of the house. The upper floor was rented out, right up until just over a year ago when Kamal got married or was married off to a girl he hardly even knew. Kamal and his young family now occupy that space. In a sense, it's still rented out because. Kamal has been paying rent to his father. Not the full amount as that which the previous tenant was paying but. It's rent payment anyway. His father said that he has got to teach the boy, (he still calls him boy even at twenty-six and married. With a second child on the way,) so he's out to teach "the boy" how to be responsible in life.

The well-manicured lawn out front was still mostly covered over with dark dirty snow and ice. The temperature has been fluctuating widely in recent times, rising and falling. But it has mostly risen significantly over the last week or so. I even saw a couple of white lilies spouting out from under the sappy fall leftover grass from last year. Those first blooming spring lilies were sprouting up along the peripheries near the ice mounds where the brown-greenish grass was already bouncing back from hibernation. I'd gotten as far as up to the granite tiles at the front door. Mr. Dahoust's words were saying. Come in, "Come in, come on in and tell us more." But his eyes were saying something quite different and very frightening.

"I really have got to be going now," I said, "Maybe some other time we can meet up when it is more convenient and more planned out. As opposed to me just dropping in on you unannounced like this."

He didn't take the hand that I'd offered.

"No, no," he protested. "You really must come on in and sit down and talk to me."

His wife, though, Luba, was a bit more civilized, than him, it would have seemed. She waved a shaking bye-bye hand at me as I turned and walked away.

"Some other time - sir," I said, "and I will come back to talk to you, but I really must go now."

That was to be the last that I was to see of Libby since then. In the same way, as I had come to know her.

On the drive back to my place downtown. I checked the phone on several occasions to verify that both sound and vibrate were active. And that it was not muted. I didn't want to miss a call; I specifically didn't want to miss Libby's call. It never came. On at least two other occasions. I'd started to dial her number but quickly decided against it and hung up. In my mind's eye, I could see her there at home being grilled by her overbearing parents, and I didn't want to be a fly on the wall when that call should come chiming in from the very person who they were there, quizzing her about.

Later that night. When I'd figured that she would probably be in bed or somehow alone by herself. I called through and nervously waited until the voicemail came in, I hung up and went to lie down. All night long I tossed and turned. I just could not find the elusive shut-eye. It was hard trying to focus on my work the following day too. I couldn't concentrate on my work. So I took the evening off, and go do a drive-by past the house at nightfall. Everything looked just as they did the night before. Everything except for the people who were there trying to figure me out. They were nowhere to be seen at this point. So, I circled around the block and came back around. Much slower this time, but still, nothing odd. I drove into the parking lot at Tim Hortons and parked. Went inside and ordered a coffee and a donut. Just the price I had to pay to hang out there. I wasn't hungry and even if I was. I had no appetite. I hung around until it began to get dark and then hopped in the truck and drove by the house again. Would have chosen to use the work truck instead of the car for more reasons than one. I went there straight from work, and I also thought that it would be much harder for me to be spotted in the truck since, other than for Libby. None of them knew about that vehicle. And thirdly, I'd figured that a work truck parked on the corner of the street in a residential neighborhood is an everyday occurrence. There's nothing strange about that.

Kamal got out of the car and was just going through the door as I approached the house. I held my head as straight as I could while still observing from the corner of my eye. He didn't go to the upstairs apartment where he was supposed to be living with his wife and child. But he went into the main dwelling instead. His mother came to the door to meet him and took one of the two brown paper bags from him that he was carrying. She then reached out and placed a hand on his waist and into the small of his back and pulled him inside. Mind you, it was just a little nudge but it was very significant for someone like me who was there searching for something, anything. Anything that could give a clue as to what might be going on, on the inside of that house, and anything that could give me a hint as to what to do or think next.

Before closing the door, Mrs. Dahoust again stuck her head slightly out the door. Looked left, then right, and then nimbly drew her face back behind the closing door. I remained put where I was sitting in the truck for another ten minutes or so. Not wanting to solicit suspicion and attention to myself there. Also, I was in the meantime, keeping my eyes open for any and every hint of what might be going on inside the house.

I eventually drove home with not much more than what I had when I arrived there. Again, that night I tried calling Libby's number but got the very same result: the party you're trying to reach is currently unavailable. Please leave a detailed message and we will get back to you shortly. Would have tried one more time before I went to sleep. Exactly the same outcome. Lying there looking up at the ceiling and trying to imagine what could have transpired behind the walls of that house. And to try to figure out what might have been going on there since Tuesday evening when I dropped her off there. Anything that could have been the cause for the cutting off of all communication so abruptly. Those things were puzzling for me. And then, suddenly, it happened. I felt the hair standing up on the back of my neck. Erectile tissues were springing to life under my nightshirt. I couldn't help but recall the tale she had told me in the conversation. When she was telling me of the incident with her brother and her, and how their father had not only almost killed him but had threatened that he would. If it ever should happen again. Looking at it from where I was lying there on my back. The situation did not seem too far removed from that one. And I could not rest in comfort. Not until I knew for sure what was going on with Libby and ensuring that she was safe. But the time was quickly slipping away.

"I've got to get going." I said to myself, "And the time to do so is now."

I ran through my notebook and agenda to see if I had jotted down any memos. Or if I had any to-do lists that might have included Libby. There was a rather vague note that I was to accompany her to Toronto or Ottawa for the interview. If and when they should call her, but nothing further. I couldn't just sit there and twiddle my thumb and do nothing. "I've got to do something," I said, but what? Just then, the demon that was lying dormant within me for way too long. Suddenly, she woke up and spoke up.

"Get busy," she said, there's a lot of work to be done, Manley.

I fired up my trusted computer and got to work. Searching for whatever. Not having a script to work with, I had to start at the beginning. The phone books. I quickly found the family. Not many Dahousts were listed in the region. So it was easy, I found her, her father Alfonso, Luba, and Kamal, living in Kirkland. No such luck with LinkedIn, Facebook, Twitter, and such. That family wasn't into the social media thing yet, it would have seemed. I hit hard against the brick wall as I thought of things to do. I concluded that the tried, tested, and true method is the best one, the hands-on one. My hands-on method. So back to the future, I had to go. I grabbed hold of my computer and my trusted toolbox containing my lock-picking apparatuses. Can't go without those on a mission like this. Welcome back to the dark side - Manley. I hopped into the truck and drove back out to Kirkland on the West Island. Drove past the Dahoust's home and parked. I then fired up my computer and got to work scanning the houses and cars for protection systems signals. While trying to pinpoint the particular ones for the Dahousts' and trying to figure out how to disable them. Did find a signal in the house. One on the Toyota Camry taxi too. That's Mr. Dahoust's car, but I did not detect any system signal on Kamal's Acura TLX sedan parked there. So, I quickly formulated a plan of action. "I'll start with the Acura," I said. It seemed like the logical choice to me because. Based on what I already knew about the family. Libby does seem to spend a lot of time in Kamal's car. So if I'm going to find anything of value? That would probably be the best place to start. Shy of getting into the house home-invasion style. This sort will probably be for a later stage in my plan if need be. I had to go and kill some more time. It was way too early for that kind of work, people were still coming and going at much too regular intervals. Two to three o'clock in the AM would be the best time to report back in for work on this shift I thought. So, I hit the road back towards downtown Montreal. In about the next four to five hours when the whole street is likely to be bedding down. I'll be back, Jack.

Chapter Eighteen: Working the Nightshift, and Overtime Too.

The clock on the night table was reporting six-thirty when I popped my eyes open the following morning. Friday morning. I propped myself up on my elbows in bed and blinked my eyes rapidly. Rubbed my hand over my eyes and stared again, at the clock. It isn't lying, it really is 6:30.

I've been missing out on a lot of sleep over the past week or so and now it is finally catching up with me. What I have to do can't wait too long. The life and welfare of my beloved Libby could be lying in the balance there. But my plan cannot be implemented under the lights of the noonday sun. So, back to the drawing board, I had to go. This is Friday Morning. Friday night is not the best night of the week for me to put the plan into effect. But it will have to suffice. I can't put this off any longer. I got to my stakeout point on the corner of the quiet street in Kirkland at exactly 12:15 AM that night into Saturday morning. I promptly set up my signal scanning system. All set, I said, let's roll. My head was down, the lion's share of my attention was focused on the computer screen when I heard it. The police car snuck up on me. There were no flashing lights, no sirens. Just that little croaking frog-like beep, beep, beep. I looked up from the computer screen, glanced at the rearview mirror, and there it was.

"Oh shit! I'm busted." Two cops got out. The one on the right quickly positioned himself on the tail end of my truck. A drawn gun in hand. The other one was carefully approaching from the left, gun in hand also.

"Good evening sir," said he. "Do you live around here?"

"No…"

"What's your purpose for sitting out here in the truck? Is this your truck…?"

More questions were coming at me than could the answers get to them, and faster than I could answer them too.

"It's my truck, yes, and I'm a computer technician," I said while reaching out to give him the business card that I had tucked in between my fingers, like, this way.

"Keep your hands where I can see them, keep your hands where I can see them," he said.

Meanwhile, the other one who was posted at the rear of the truck quickly filled my right-side window and promptly cracked at the door latch. It didn't budge. The other officer grabbed hold of the other door handle. Pulling and screaming, "Get out of the vehicle, get out of the vehicle."

I unlocked the door and slid out. They bounced my face up against the truck, twisting my arms in the most unnatural ways possible, as the handcuffs were being clamped on. They didn't read me any rights like one might see in the movie. But this was not a movie, this was a real-life setting baby. And the pain and fear I was feeling right at that moment were as real as it gets in real life. They pushed my head down and squeezed me into the back seat of the police car.

"Where are you taking me?" I asked.

"Down to the station for starters," he replied. "And then where we go from here will be dependent on how cooperative you turn out to be."

"What will become of my truck?" I asked several minutes later when we were about halfway to the station as it turned out.

"It will probably be towed by tomorrow this time, unless…"

"Unless what?" I had to ask this several minutes later when it became clear that there was no intention of him finishing the hanging statement.

"It all depends on how cooperative you turn out to be, what answers you have for these troubling questions floating around in the air," said the sergeant. "And which needs to be answered."

"It's all a misunderstanding," I said, after the preliminary questions that were designed to ID me.

"So, Mr. Techno man, try to make me understand here. Tell me, what's the story, what's the real story?"

"Like I said before, sir. I'm a technician, amongst other things."

"What other things, what else do you do? Home invasion? Stalking people in their homes? What is it?"

"Can I speak a word in your ear, your ears only?" I said to the Sergeant, he didn't speak, just fanned him away - the young constable. With a little bit of waving movement of the hand. The constable, to his credit, had started to clear out of the office as soon as I'd said that I wanted to talk to the Sergeant, alone.

"Here's the deal", I said when we were left alone. "I cut right through to the chase and give you what you're looking for. I'll tell you what is going down. And you, give me a break with this interrogation bit. And let me go get my truck and get on home."

"Is that it?"

"Well, one more thing, keep me updated on whatever you may find out. Perhaps?"

"No, oh no, that I cannot do. Police work is a serious business - Jack."

"Okay, okay I got you. But I want you to understand that there might be people's lives at risk here. People that I care greatly about."

"So, start talking, I'm listening."

"You'd ask me what I was doing over there. The truth is. I was doing your job, sort of. I do believe that someone is in that house who is in trouble, and I wanted to be sure it was so before I go on to make an alarm."

"Who's this person? This "someone" of whom you speak?"

"A friend of mine, Libby, is her name."

"What kind of friend are we talking about here, are you seeing her?"

"Sort of, it's not official yet but we have been getting really tight of late. But her family is very controlling and overbearing, and..."

"Hang on right there, I'll be back." The sergeant went and got the constable to join us again. After whispering things into his ear, and then, he got on the phone and called for another to get to the station as soon as possible.

The Sergeant's instructions to his two subordinates were to put twenty-four-seven surveillance in effect on this particular house and then lay low and watch. "Keep track of all activities and goings-on," he said.

Left alone with me. The sergeant reached across the table. Got his notepad and started writing as I told him in detailed terms what I knew and when. It was well after sunrise when I walked up to my truck still parked there on the corner and hopped in. I was sure that authoritative eyes were somewhere close by watching my every move. I was rather confident that we were on the same team by then though. I cranked up the engine and delayed much longer than I needed to in the pretend engine warm-up routine. When I couldn't prolong the act any longer. I pulled out and drove home to my place in the downtown core of Montreal.

Chapter Nineteen: Breaking News and Reports.

Monday morning at 8:15 AM on the dot. The phone rang. It was the Sergeant's private number he had given me before I had to skip the joint in the wee hours of that morning. "Got some news for you," he said. "First the good news. We've found your girlfriend, but the bad news is. She's in bad shape."

"Where is she, can I talk to her?"

"No, no, you can't talk to her nor can you see her anytime soon. You cannot talk to anybody connected to her either. Not her parents, not her brother, not anyone. Not until I give you the okay, -okay?"

"Is she going to be, like, okay? How bad is this bad news of which you speak?"

"She'll be okay-Buddy, she'll be okay soon. Just keep calm and go look after yourself. Try to be your best self against that day when she may need you."

"And how's her family, what about her parents, where are they?"

"I can't divulge those pieces of information. That will be all for now. If and when I have further information, I will be in touch with you-okay?"

"It's not okay Serge., but what can I do? You're the boss here-right?"

"Take care, Manley."

"Bye-Sir."

The sergeant might not be able to tell me what I want to know. But this is still a free country and the wide-open road leads to Libby's door.

And that's just where I'm going, not when the officer gets back to me. Not tomorrow, but now. Right away, right this minute.

I fired up the car engine and hit the road west towards Kirkland. Drove right by the Dahoust's home, circled the block, and came back around. There weren't any signs of life in the main dwelling area where Libby lived with her family. But there seemed to be a light and some movement upstairs and both vehicles were still parked up there in the driveway. I didn't stop or linger. Just passed by on the drive, in, and out again. I needed to dig in a bit further. So I drove into the Tim Horton's parking lot and parked. Went inside and ordered something to eat. I picked out a particular girl sitting by herself at a table across from me. A young woman with auburn hair, blue eyes, and a shape to die for. A perky pair of breasts. Just a tad on the small side, but a proper mouthful for someone like Mr. Puppy-dog here to nibble on. She seemed likable too. A friendly outgoing type, and she did give me an eye for a time or two while I was at the counter placing my order.

"Care if I join you?" I asked when I approached the table where she was sitting. Holding on tightly to the tray in my hand.

"Sure," she said, "go ahead." So, I pulled out the chair and sat down across from her.

"You from around here?" She inquired through a gluttonous burger bite.

"No, just kind of passing through, and you? Do you live around here?"

"Hmm-um," she nodded and shook her head, "all my life. I was born and brought up here on the west island, not too far from here as a matter of fact."

"So, you happen to know anything about what was supposed to have happened around these parts yesterday? Or last night? I hear a lot of talk about some police operations and such the likes."

"Hmm-um," she nods, shaking her head again. "...A girl who went against her family's wishes and was dating some guy that they didn't approve of, they held her hostage in her own home for days. Weeks, maybe, without food and all. The cops got word of it and busted in on them. Freeing the girl and locking up the parents. As well as the brother whom they say was aiding and abetting them. And some other guy, a taxi driver or something like that, another one who was to have gotten himself caught up in the whole mess."

"So where is the girl now, any word on her whereabouts?"

"In the hospital, I would guess, they'd said that she needed urgent medical attention, and fast..."

I glanced at my watch, "oh-oh! I've got to go back to work. Can't keep burning money even before you get it in your hands, can you?"

"What manner of work is it that you do again?"

"I'm a technician, computer technician," I replied on the walk outside. She trotted out the door behind me, obviously yearning for more.

"Can I call you sometime?" She asked. "Is there a number I can reach you at, or something?"

"I don't think that would be such a good idea," I said, as I opened up the door and hopped in. Closing the door behind me. She furrowed her brow and stared at me in wonderment. Had it been any other time in my life? I'd be banging hard on her wide-open door in a New York minute. Even if it was like, while I was still married to Aylene or any other time. Up until a couple of months ago when I started to talk to Libby, and not just watching her from a distance. If it had been any other time up until then that I was to have happened upon this girl. In a setting like this. I'd be squeezing my way in and out of her pants in those said types of metropolitan time measures. And be done gone long before someone (anyone at all) could say: you slimy little puppy dog you. But there's a fork that suddenly popped up in front of me on the road. I got derailed off the track I was previously on. Where does this new road lead from here? I have no concrete idea, but...

Chapter Twenty: Get on the Move, Now.

On the second evening of the stakeout. Saturday evening. Two officers were sitting in the lookout vehicle. A Ford club wagon, at some point around 7:20 PM, when the darkness was beginning to settle in properly. They spotted a U-Haul moving truck rolling up and halted to a stop in front of the Dahoust family home. Kamal was the driver. He got out of the vehicle carrying a duffle bag that he swung over his shoulder and went inside.

The lights flash twice to indicate that the vehicle is securely locked up and will probably activate the alarm system. Immediately the constable dialed up the Sergeant's number.

"Action, action," he said. "We've got activities going on at the location. Some sort of moving truck has just pulled up and parked in front of the house."

"Okay, got you, keep your ears and eyes peeled. We can't afford to miss anything. I'll be there soon."

They were so very surprised to see the senior cop not more than five minutes later driving by. In a regular police car. Normally he would have used an unmarked car for this type of fact-finding mission, but then again. Maybe it wasn't so much a fact-finding mission that the Sergeant was on in his mind, not yet at least. He probably just wanted to reassure the guys that he was really on the job and that he had got them all covered.

He could have also wanted to make it appear as normal as possible. It's just a patrol car doing the rounds in a quiet, upscale neighborhood. Nothing to be alarmed about in that, nothing at all. For the rest of the night. Everything remained quiet and calm. Yes, there were obvious activities on the inside of the house but nothing it would seem that was not consistent with the rhythm of life in a normal household. Come the following morning, however. The activity was revved up by several degrees. Of course, there was a move in the making, a big move. They were loading up the truck with household items, everything from beds, tables, and chairs. On through to clothing and kitchen wares. It was Kamal and another young man who was busily lugging the stuff. One whom the cops were not able to properly ID from where they were sitting in their lab van. Every now and again the older Dahoust man would come outside bearing a small item or two. At other times, it seemed like he would just bring instructions to the two workhorses and then leave.

On two separate points. The madam, Mrs. Luba Dahoust, came to the door and stuck her head outside as if to look at the happenings. But on both occasions, before returning inside to the safety of the house. She would do what had by then become a sort of defining signature-like, look up, look down the road ritual before pulling herself back behind the closing door.

As soon as the truck loading activities were to have gotten started. The officer called back to the base and to the Sergeant. "Get ready for action," he said, "real action. The truck is being loaded, as we speak."

"Got you," the sergeant acknowledged the info. "You guys did very well. Be there in a flash…" "Stay calm and covered, no need for rushing it now."

That was an understatement. The understatement of the decades that was, in the cop's minds. As it turned out though. The Sergeant's decision to take things slowly was what led to a further collection of ironclad evidence that would solidify their case and prove beyond all reasonable doubt what was taking place. Or what was about to take place within the family and the household in general. It was also good enough to help them in putting the guilty parties away for long stretches.

Because these two officers have been working on the stakeout continuously for a couple of days on end. The sergeant had to arrange a change of shift. Five officers came riding in the blue Chevrolet Express van and all, but one were armed and equipped for action. One exception in the bunch was Corporal Weir. Other than for his service revolver that he was carrying concealed. He bears no other resemblance to being a cop on duty. He was there to drive the other vehicle back. The Ford Club Wagon with two other overworked and tired officers. The other four who came with him were in the newly deployed vehicle. They were there to pick up from where those two had left off. Be alert and ready for action at any given moment.

They'd dropped him off (Corporal Weir that is,) on the corner of the street. On the corner of St Charles and Brunswick boulevards, he walked in from there and approached the Ford van, shaking a bunch of keys in his right hand on the approach. He inserted the key into the lock and opened up the door, or at least. He acted in those parts as a disguise to the would-be eyewitness. Since the other two cops were already inside the vehicle. All the while expecting him to show up. And laying low in the vehicle in order to maintain their cover. He wasted no time, acting as normal as he could. He started the engine and then hesitated just long enough to make it appear to anyone who might be looking on that, this was someone who just came back to pick up a vehicle that had been parked there on the corner for a while. With the other two cops still lying low inside the vehicle, he drove away.

Meanwhile, one street away. But while still in plain view of the front door of the house and of the moving truck that was parked in front of that house. The blue Chevrolet Express van was strategically parked there. With four freshly deployed cops sitting inside it. Alert and ready to pounce. Other police vehicles were also strategically deployed and were circulating on nearby streets in the area. All the while being in continuous, up-to-the-minute communication with those cops in the lookout van and with the Sergeant.

Nightfall and activities step up a notch. The lawmen could feel it. Something was about to go down and they did not want to blink a heavy eyelid. Lest they miss out on something important.

At 1:20 AM the activities became visible in the Dahousts' household, the dim light, the moving around, and then. Then came the car that pulled up and stopped right behind the moving truck, a taxicab. It seemed like one from the same company where Mr. Dahoust works. However, the cops were monitoring what was going on within the house. Both visually and electronically. Yet they did not pick up on the call for a taxi. Did they mess up on that? How could they? How could they have missed that one? The front door cracked open partially, and Mr. Dahoust came to the door and looked outside. Apparently, to verify that it was the cab that he had ordered. Seemingly satisfied with what he had seen. He pushed back the door and left it somewhat ajar as he walked back inside and tarried there for a while. The cabbie did not get out of the vehicle, not at once anyway. He remains seated until…

The door opened up again, much wider than before. There were more people there in the passageway too. At this point. A little dim light appeared in the taxi, (the roof light probably.) The cabbie cracked the door open and slid out. He walked up to the front door and placed a hand under one of the woman's arms on the other side of the elder Dahoust male who was baring up the other side of the woman. They slowly walked her back to the taxi and eased her in.

Although the female figure whom they escorted out of the house and into the car, looked rather shaky from the officer's standpoint, they could not see her facial outline because. She was wearing a scarf that covered her head, and most of her face. Then draped down over her shoulders. Her right hand was holding the scarf in place with a grip just under the chin. The cops knew it was not Mrs. Luba Dahoust, because. She had just appeared in the doorway and returned inside, and there was no other evidence, either by way of statistical research or via their surveillance. To suggest that there was another woman figure living in the house except for Kamal's wife Selma who lives on the upper floor. And she's a much smaller statue than this individual in the picture.

This leads them to the only logical conclusion that: this is in fact, their subject. The daughter and sister of the Dahousts, and the friend of their aid, Manley. This was, in fact, Libby.

Again, the instructions came from the big boss: the sergeant. "Stay put, don't move in yet." To the chagrin of most, if not all of his subordinates.

"This is it, what more is he waiting for?" Asked one of the cops. "Until the girl drops dead? Which could be any minute now from the looks of things." Said another of the mildly frustrated cops in the surveillance vehicle. But time alone was to prove that again the senior cop was spot on right. The next figure to show up on the scene was none other than the girl's brother, Kamal. He tumbled out the door on the top floor and skipped on down the winding wrath iron staircase that leads down from the upstairs apartment, he was still fumbling with the (seemingly) faulty zipper head on the bottom of the overcoat, look, there. He got it set and pulled the slider all the way up to close the coat under his throat.

The lights flashed on the moving truck as he unlocked the door via remote mechanisms and hopped in. He started up the engine and then slid back out, walked up to the taxicab, and had a few words with the driver. The taxi then drove away as Kamal walked back to the front door of the house and knocked. His father came and opened up the door. Standing in the passageway with Kamal standing on the front doorstep. They exchanged words, after which Kamal went back into the truck and drove off in the same direction as the taxicab before him...

Chapter Twenty-one: Sly Spy Family Mission.

The white Isuzu cube truck was parked alongside the store in Cote des Neige. I knew he was there. I put on my disguise and walked into the store, passed his mother there at the counter tending to a customer. With a couple of other customers standing in line behind her. I spotted Kamal near the rear of the store stocking shelves. He didn't recognize me of course because of my disguise and the act that I was putting on. A Russian-style winter hat. Definitely too warm for the current temperature type of gear. An oversized scarf around my neck, and a pair of ridiculous-looking reading glasses. That was my second trip inside the store for the day. As I approached him, I was coughing into the crooks of my sleeve - a cough, cough, coughing.

"Hi," I said, coughing, "can you help me out here? I need to find a bottle of Ferrol compound, good for coughs and colds I was told." Cough, cough. This is the perfect camouflage for me. I'll be using it to enhance my disguise. I'll surely be coughing a lot when I get up to the counter too. Kamal pointed the weird stranger (me) to the shelf around the bend.

I had gone in and out of there before. That was, to seek out the farthest, most discreet corner where I could talk to Kamal alone without being seen or overheard by the mother. So it wasn't by coincidence that I had chosen to ask for the Ferrol compound.

Once we were standing there in front of the shelf where the items were stacked. I started dismantling my disguise. "Look." I said, "I'm here to talk to you privately and quickly. So, keep it down as much as you can, and let's get it over and done with, will you?"

"What's this about?" He asked. A cold and frightened look now suddenly plastered on his face.

"Libby, it's about Libby," I said rather directly. "Where's she, what happened to her?"

"She, she, Libby is on her way to India... At this very moment as a matter of fact. She's to be married to someone there in a few weeks."

"India eh! It had better be so, because, if not? I can be your worst nightmare. You see, Kamal, I know a lot about you, and them, your parents. And when I say "a lot?" I mean an awful lot. And I do know how to use what I know and use it, I will. So, for your sake my friend, I do hope that you're telling me the truth here. Strange though it may seem to you now." I said this as I was planting a firm and heavy right hand on his slumping shoulder. While I was replacing my disguises afterward, I added: "I'll be heading back to base now to start the process of verifying your claims."

...

I was early on the scene, but not as early as he was. Kamal was already there. He arrived in the truck and backed up into the alleyway to get to the delivery door. I saw it all starting at this point when I had turned the corner three blocks down. I moved into position, parked, and sat in my car, and then zoomed in with my spy-lensed eyes on what was happening as it went down. He slid like the slime ball he is, out of the truck and hopped around it to get to the side door of the store.

Having a bunch of keys in his hand he went and opened up the door and entered inside. After about fifteen anxious minutes. Anxious on my part, that is. While he was inside the building, and hence, out of the scope of my vision, I waited. He came back outside by way of the rear delivery door, then proceeded to open up the push-up garage-type door on the tail end of the truck and climb in. I could not see him anymore from where I was sitting inside my car and watching the scene. But I'd assumed that he was moving around. Or shifting the products down closer to the tail end of the vehicle in order to get them out of there. I was right.

He climbed back down off the tail end of the truck and proceeded to move cardboard boxes from the truck to the store by way of the same back door out of which he had come earlier. Just then, a young man came by and greeted him. He then promptly joined in on the unloading task.

Next, there was the taxicab. Mr. Dahoust's motorized workhorse had arrived. Bringing along Mrs. Luba Dahoust, his wife and mother of his children, with him. They both got out and went to the back of the truck and exchanged words with Kamal. They didn't seem to even so much as to take notice that the other young man was there. Let alone to have greeted him. And then both of them turned and went inside the store. Both the man and his wife. Leaving the other two young men to carry on with the task of unloading the truck. I used that open window of opportunity to pull out of the spot where I was parked in a position parallel to both the store and the delivery truck they were unloading. I did this without being noticed by them. I was more than sure. I then circled around the block and came back to park plumb in front of the store, where I sat and waited until the store finally opened up properly for business. I also watched as Mr. Dahoust climbed back into his car and drove away about five minutes later. Off to work I'd assumed. I remain seated for about another five or six minutes and then. When I saw that there were enough people who had gone inside of the store to do their various business there. I knew that, that would have certainly been enough of them to provide sufficient cover for me as I go about running my sly spy errands. Having all those bases now covered. I went inside and pointed my nose towards the farthest corner of the shopping spaces on the floor. Far away from the direct prying eyes of the proprietors. I spotted the target there. Or maybe it was the target that had spotted me since I did not know beforehand what I was going in there to look for or to pick up. However, it was that unique item that just stood out in my eyes and in my memory. It also happened to be something that could fit perfectly well into my undercover spy plan.

It was a blue cardboard box containing the bottle of Ferrol compound. I turned around and walked briskly back outside. All the while, I was being careful to keep my empty hands in plain view so as not to be soliciting any suspicion from anyone. Or risking a chance of me being mistaken by them for being a shoplifter, and hence, cause unnecessary problems. At the same time, I was keeping my face as far from their view and as disfigured and out of shape as possible. So that they would not be able to recognize me. Be it at the present time or at some other time in the future. Like, when I shall return in the next couple of minutes for example.

I then hopped back into the car and drove away, doing the rounds yet again. I looped back around the street and then stopped. Almost at the same place where I was parked for the first time while I was watching the unloading go down. That exact spot was taken by another vehicle by then, however, just across from there. There was an open slot on the other side of the road, so I parked there. I then set about re-arranging my attire and hence, my appearance. By putting on another disguise, the oversized coat, and a scarf. Another "too-hot-for-the-current temperature Russian winter hat. And the fake reading glasses that I had picked up at the dollar store the other day. I was already burning up, but a man has got to do what a man has got to do, right? So, I returned to the store and headed straight to the point where I already knew that I would find the Ferrol compound. I was way too hot in my camouflage outfit to be dilly-dallying around fake shopping. Just go in and get it done and out again. The rest, as they say, is history.

Chapter Twenty –two: On the Move, Again.

Seven police service vehicles were deployed along the route from St Charles Boulevard, and on through to the Trans-Canada highway west side towards the Ontario border. Strategically situated at points where one might possibly get off the road and turn around or change course. This was put into effect by the sergeant after the taxicab was to have moved out with the woman inside. The body temperature of all the officers occupying these units was way up. At any minute a call to action could come.

Upon the approach to the bridge. At the last exit on the Montreal side of the river. The taxicab exited Highway 40 West and parked on the down ramp near the underpass. All of that info was relayed to the man in command. Then, when Kamal and the moving truck pulled out and left. All of the police units looped up behind him. From a distance of course. So, he never knew that he was being followed until...

"Green lights," said the sergeant, "go get them." The truck had just exited the highway at the very same point where the taxicab had gotten off and parked. Coincidence? Very possible. Was it a real happenstance though? Highly improbable. Argued the senior cop. Based on what they have seen thus far. And because the woman in the car was, seemingly, in some sort of distress when they'd put her in. The sergeant did not want to prolong the time further before he could get her help or get her to the hospital to be checked out properly. Furthermore, the picture that presented itself so far left little doubt in his mind as to what was going down. The two vehicles were then circled by police cars. Sirens were heard in the distance as more cops and probably an ambulance were on the approach.

"What is the purpose of you being parked up here?" The officer asked the cabbie.

"I was waiting for someone."

"Who might that someone be?" May I ask?

"The gentleman in the truck behind you."

"Is the lady 'okay?'"

"I don't know sir, why don't you ask her that?" She can speak for herself. I just picked her up back there a while ago."

"Miss," the officer called out to the woman across the driver's face but she didn't respond.

She looked distant and incoherent to the cop. He walked around to the other side of the vehicle and tried again to talk to the woman but still got no response other than a slight turn of the head to look in his direction and back again.

He got on the radio and called the Sergeant.

"Serge. I think we need to get help for the woman as soon as possible."

"Coming right up," the sergeant responded.

Meanwhile, with Kamal now in the truck, behind the taxicab. The sergeant wasn't wasting time. He asked the young man just a few further questions before giving instructions to the officer to cuff him and take him for a ride back down to the station too. He wasn't in the mood to be wasting any more time out of the office on this case. The same instructions were given to the other officers in regard to the rest of the family at the house.

Everybody has got their man (or woman,) depending on which one. Libby was taken off to the hospital. Kamal and the cabbie to the police lockup.

The Sergeant has got a call or two more to make. On the drive back toward St Charles Boulevard and Kirkland. Well after daybreak. He took out his cell phone and placed a call through…

Meanwhile, back at the family home in Kirkland. Three separate vehicles were being loaded up with: the father, and the mother, and from the upstairs apartment came the pregnant wife of Kamal and her young son. A call was placed through to the child protection services to come and get the young child if necessary. The hospital also said the search was on, in earnest for fresh emergency room staffing. A poison and toxicology unit was also called in.

Chapter Twenty —three: Family Reunion.

While he was being escorted out of the police car in the parking lot at the police station. Kamal caught a glimpse of his father and mother in the reception area by way of the partly frosted-partly plain glasses at the front of the building. They were accompanied by several police officers around them. Mr. Dahoust was standing in front of the counter with both hands held in front of him in a downward position as if he was wearing handcuffs. His wife, Luba, who was sitting in a chair close by, had her head hung down, and both hands in her lap as if she might be confined by the same sort of restraining devices too. They took Kamal into a separate room and sat him down. Get ready for the long-haul Kamal, the rush is now on. For real.

...

The police had theorized that. The evening after she got home from the movies with Manley. A man who didn't in any way fit into their idea of a suitor for their daughter. That was to have triggered anger and rage in the father and then. Libby's firmness and steadfast assertiveness in defending her right to choose who she was going to marry and spend the rest of her life with. This left the rest of the family stupefied and so enraged that they probably inflicted blows on her. Which spelled trouble for them from the get-go, so they went to work trying to cover their tracks by finishing her off.

They had also gone to Ontario at some earlier point and would have signed off on the lease agreement she had secured for the apartment.

This was done supposedly on her behalf since she was too occupied elsewhere to make the trip, in conforming to their theory. The follow-up plan was to have her body placed in the moving truck. Most likely around the steering wheel and in the driver's seat and have it plunged into the river, one way or another. But then, this Manley fellow keeps sticking his nose where it didn't belong, in their deranged minds. And maybe they had noticed an increase in vehicular activity and police presence in the neighborhood. All of that was to serve to further spook them into an attempt to expedite the process. To their own undoing and hopefully, in the girl's interests and to her benefit. If she is not yet too far gone to be able to recover from the ordeal.

...

The sergeant said that Libby was in the hospital, He could not tell me more than that, not yet he'd said. Well, I could not just sit down there and do nothing. I went to the mother of all the hospitals in Montreal: the Montreal General Hospital and inquired around as much as I could. But the general consensus I came away with was that she was not there, not at that hospital. So, my next stop was to be at the hospital in her own neighborhood and closer to her home in Kirkland. Or thereabouts. That, as it turned out, was the lakeshore general hospital. I thought to myself, maybe she's not as bad as they are making it out to be. Maybe they can handle it there at the local health facility. Bingo, I was right. Although they did not come out and admit forthrightly that she was there? It was more like: "Who are you? Are you related to her? This is a police case. We can't let any and everyone in to see her, just family."

"I am a 'family,'" I said, "She's my girlfriend," hoops. I bit my lip. I should have said, my fiancé. I might have stood a far better chance of getting through to them. But there was no doubt in my mind that she was there. Whatever I have to do thereafter, to get them to allow me to see her. That was what I was going to do next. I didn't tarry there much longer after I found out where she was, sort of. I headed back in the direction of home. I needed to redirect my efforts and energy toward figuring out how to get to Libby herself and how to get her out of there.

On the way home I made a small detour through Cote des Neige. And pass by the shop. It was closed for sure. The Isuzu pickup truck was parked by the side. I did see a number of people standing in front of the closed doors. A few of them, (women in conference,) were chatting away. Think I had a fairly good idea of what the conversation was all about.

One man walked past the females there at the conference and went to pull on the door. Rather aggressively I thought to myself. Before turning around and walking away cursing under his breath. Upon realizing (belatedly though it was) that the store was closed. I drove away and continued on home.

Chapter Twenty-four: Vigil for My Valentine.

Valentine's Day February 14th it was. I picked up a bouquet of flowers and went to the hospital. I've been showing up there almost every day for over a week since I discovered that she was there. The pretty little receptionist knows me by name now, and she seemed to be warming up to me somewhat too. "I would really like her to have these," I told her. "I think this would brighten up her day if nothing else." I was prepared to give it to her to get it to Libby, but I had to try first. Peradventure she would let me go in and see her. Valentine's Day was my lucky day as it turned out. But it didn't come without a good deal of tests and trials, and the patience of a modern-day type of Job.

"Have a seat," she said, "let me see if I can work out something for you."

She got on the phone and dialed up somebody. Who? Did you ask? How would I know who? They talked for a minute, then she hung up and called someone else, nothing. Then another, and another. She must have called and talked to twenty, perhaps twenty-five people before...

The minutes turned into hours... I was beginning to get really tired and hungrier by the minute. And then I overheard her telling someone: "he has been coming here every day for over a week now. Begging for a chance to see her."

I thought that was rather generous of her because. I did miss out on a couple of days here and there. I then watched rather amusingly as a couple of heads came popping out from behind a door jamb and pulled back a few times after they were done scrutinizing me for a brief moment.

Meanwhile, I was just sitting there waiting, hoping and praying, until...

One lady came to the desk and sat down next to the receptionist who by then was fast becoming my forever best friend. A lifesaver she will forever be in my mind because of the way things started unfolding since she took an active approach to help me. The new lady appearing in the picture called me up to the window and started questioning me in the same way as if I were a would-be patient. While scribbling away at the information provided, on parchment. At other times, those questions took on an airy and uncanny resemblance to those that the police were asking me a while back. She wanted to know: my name, my occupation, home, and business addresses, and what was the relation-ship between the patient and me. What living arrangements do I have or share with others? And the list goes on. However, deep inside my guts, I was beginning to get the feeling that I was being taken seriously, for once. And that I now stand a good chance of getting to see Libby. And that was to make everything well worth it for me from then on.

The good lady then turned to me and said: "I'm going to talk to the patient, to see how she feels about all of this. If she'll see you, you're good to go, but if not, I'm afraid, I can't allow you to go in. This will be all up to her. Do you understand?"

"I... I totally understand and agree with that. That will be a lot more than I have been hoping for, for over a week now." I hastened to add.

"I'll be back," she said, "have a seat in the waiting room."

"Today is your lucky day," said that lady upon her return twenty minutes or so later, "she will see you."

Shiue! I exhaled as I reached over and across to the other chair, grabbed the bouquet, and followed the good lady along the corridor that leads to the elevator. And up to the intensive care unit. Libby saw me on the approach, she sat up on the bed and stretched out both arms towards me as my steps hastened to get to her. We embraced. She, sit-ting up in the bed and leaning sideways towards me kneeling there by the bedside and leaning in, cried, and sobbed for a while, of course. Not me, no, I didn't cry, but she did. The lady, though, I still am not sure if she was a doctor. Or a nurse, an orderly, or whatever her role there was, but for those few hours that our paths happened to cross. She was my angel of mercy. Our angel of mercy.

They allowed me to spend the rest of that night there with Libby in the room. We talked about what had happened to her. As much of it as she could remember. I told her about some of the troubles I ran into in trying to get information and leads to get to her. She seemed well enough to me, to be getting out of there soon. But she said she didn't know where she was going to live because she would not be going back to live with her parents. I didn't tell her that her parents were no longer there. Didn't think it was time to tell her what had happened to them. Or even if it was my role to tell her about such things. It seemed to me like no one told her anything.

"I'll be here for you - Lib," I assured her. "Comes what may, I'm here for you."

...

Medical reports stated that a number of substances were found in her system. From traces of sleeping pills to something resembling windshield washer fluid. The findings were sent out to labs for further testing. At least one other unidentified substance was detected and isolated and sent off for further testing too, I was told. Until they are able to say for sure what those substances are and are able to get an idea of how those may interact with the medications that she's given or will be given. As to how such may affect or interact with her overall long-term health. She will remain in the intensive care unit where she is being closely monitored.

...

Libby came home.

"How am I ever going to be able to tell Libby about it, in her current state? Like, what had happened to her parents?" I was shaking in my boots as I parked the car in the parking lot at the Lakeshore General Hospital and got out. I was there on a big date. I was going there to take Libby back home with me. Yes, everything was arranged for her to come home and stay with me to continue her recovery from a home setting rather than to be in the hospital. I was beginning to get the feeling by then though, that she knew something about what had happened to her parents. I was hoping that I was right on the mark with that one too because. I was petrified at the mere thought of what might happen, or what I would do. If it turned out that I would have to be the one to break the news to her, on my own, in the apartment. While she's supposed to be there to recover and regain her strength. I most certainly wasn't looking forward to that.

The discourse has been changing of late though, when it comes to her parents. It was more like what is it that you're not telling me. Where are they? As opposed to, did they come when I was asleep? Or when are they coming?

...

"So, when were you going to tell me?" She asked me in the car while on the way home from the hospital.

"What are you talking about?" I asked a minute later.

"I already know, Manley. So, you don't have to go pussyfooting around the issue."

"How did you learn about it, who told you?" I asked her again after an even longer minute's pause.

"People are talking, I overheard things. And a little bird pecked me and told me a few more things."

"How few is 'few' here? How much did this little bird tell you?"

"...That they were arrested and charged for..."

She didn't bother to finish the sentence.

You shouldn't get yourself too worked up. Relax. We can talk more about it later.

"I'm alright, I'm doing quite fine, I'm okay, thank you."

"Whoa, whoa, don't bite my head off over this Lib. I couldn't just waltz on in there while you were lying on a recovery bed, bearing bad news to you. Especially, not that type of bad news."

"Are you okay?" I again asked the oxymoronic question of the day.

Look at her there in the back seat. She's almost as pretty as I have come to know her. But every now and then she would wince and grimace. She was in obvious discomfort.

"Let's make a deal," I said to her "You tell me exactly what you're going through. How you are feeling, where it hurts, and the like. And I? I'll tell you everything that I know about your parents and whatever else that has been happening. Deal? Deal?" I asked again, insisting on an answer, something like a verbal agreement, perhaps. Okay! She agreed.

...

"Did you not receive any of my calls and messages?" I asked. "I tried to contact you several times that evening after I dropped you home and left. And then, I also left a voice message or two sometime afterward."

She wasn't responding to many of my queries, but I had to hold up my end of the deal. She had told me her side of the story. What little she could remember of it, at least. And in keeping with my promise to her, I had to tell her what I knew, and when.

"...I couldn't sleep that night" I continued. "So, I had to think of something to do. And then go get it done fast. I did a little bit of re-search here and there and then went back out to Kirkland on a mission to investigate. I didn't find much on that occasion, but I wasn't going to quit. I made several trips out there, both before and after..." Stop.

"Before and after what?" She wanted to know.

"I got busted by the cops."

"Got busted? What for?"

"Long story, and one that I'm not proud to talk about."

"What did you do? Did you hurt someone?"

"Not quite. I was stalking the house, your house."

"Stalking our house? What for?"

"Just trying to see if there was anything that I could find out. After what had happened in the evening when I had dropped you home there. And after several failed attempts at contacting you, I couldn't just sit around and do nothing you know. I went back out there on a 'spy mission.' You know, like, to mine for information. I was in the work truck setting up my surveillance system when the cops snuck up from behind and busted me and then took me down to the police station for questioning. I almost crapped my pants when I heard the beepers from behind me. And then those two cops started mishandling me." She was laughing, yes, Libby was sitting there laughing at me, what a beautiful sight. It was almost like the Libby I had come to know. That contagious laughter, she's back. I said to myself, Libby's back. Or is she?

...

"So what happened, you got locked up for stalking me? For stalking our house?"

"No, I would have managed to talk myself out of it. Out of spending at least a night in jail."

"Yes? I'm sure you did. A man of many great and convincing words, no? Good for you."

"I just told them what I knew."

"What did you tell them?" She asked after an extended pause.

"Just the facts... As I knew them." Another pause. "I told them. Well, I told the sergeant in particular. I told him that I had a friend in the house whom I thought was in some sort of danger and that I was there trying to verify that that was the case before I went on to make an alarm. He must have had reasons to believe me because without any further hesitation. He was to venture into implementing a round-the-clock watch on the house. And on its occupants. Then after picking my brain for whatever else, he could harvest. He then turned me loose so that I could go get my truck and go home. That was Friday night into Saturday morning. Three days or so after we last saw each other. The sergeant then warned me off, telling me to stay away from the whole thing and leave it up to the cops to do their job. On Sunday night though, well. Monday morning it was. On Monday morning, early, the call came in from the Sergeant, as he had promised me. He had promised me as part of the deal that he would get in touch with me if and when there was something to tell me. So, he called and told me that they had found you (the good news.) But the bad news was that you were in bad shape and were in need of immediate medical attention. That was when my second round of investigations kicked in... I needed more information. "Serge" was rather lean on the details. Said I must focus on taking care of myself against the day when you might need me. Rather sweet I thought but I wasn't in the mood for sweetness. I was way past that at this juncture. 'It's action time now,' I said while rising up from where I was lying on my bed at home. I needed answers. And I needed them fast. I went back out to Kirkland for yet another stakeout and more. That was when I learned that the whole family, except for your brother's wife, of course. What's her name again?"

"Selma."

"Yes, Selma, she was the only one not locked up and was there at the house alone with her child. And then there was to be some speculation going around that you were in the hospital. I launched Operation Hospital Search, in an effort at finding you since everybody seemed tight-lipped about your whereabouts. From the cops to the hospital staff. Nobody was talking. However, I did my research and eventually found you at Lakeshore General Hospital. I then had to be very vigilant and persistent from there, until. I suppose they got a bit tired of me and so, they came clean. Well, the rest of it, from that point on, you now know."

"What did you tell them?"

"Tell who?"

"At the hospital, what did you tell them in order to get them to let you in?"

"A number of things, in fact, I said, (rather foolishly I think). I told them that you were my girlfriend. Think that ended up doing more harm to my cause than good. I should have thought a bit more about it before answering, like a fool… In the end though. I think I might have just worn them out and into submission. They probably thought that I would just keep on showing up and sitting in on them, day after day until they gave up, and I would. So they gave in. Adding to the fact that nobody else was showing up there on your behalf. In terms of the family that is. All that must have played a role in their decision to let me in to see you. But not before they grilled me thoroughly, like a common criminal being probed by the cops. At one point. I thought that they were going to ask me which hand I use to wipe my backside after using the toilet. I was ready and waiting to tell them that 'I use tissues. Five or more squares of double-ply toilet tissue. Not with my hands, neither of the two. Like those people that you know and associate yourselves with seemed to be accustomed to doing.' But by the time I got there, to that part? I was beginning to get the feeling that we were on the brink of a major breakthrough. I was going to get my chance to see you after all. I was right."

...

It was hard to get her (Libby) talking but once she got started, there was no stopping her, well, except for...

She doesn't remember much of what had happened from that first night at the house. Up to the point where she found herself waking up in the hospital. She remembered though, getting into a fight with her parents over the issue of her going out with me. As soon as she got in the house, she said. Her father pounced on her. Verbally abusing her, name-calling, and telling her not to see that "boy" again, ever.

"You're going to marry someone decent, honorable, and noble. Not some piece of trash that you go pick up somewhere to come dragging in on this family. We're going to get you a nice and decent young man who will uphold the family honor."

"You're not going to do any such thing, not for me. I countered them on that. I can and will find my own suitor. My own mate. You are not going to be playing matchmaker for me as you did with Kamal." She argued against them. The argument became loud and boisterous. "Out of the corner of my eye. I saw Mom come through the kitchen door with a pot. Or a frying pan. Or something like that in her hand. I felt the blow over my head that sent me flying to the floor. The next thing I remember after that was. I woke up bound and gagged in the basement. How long was I there? I had no idea. Mom came with food and tried to get me to eat something, but I wasn't hungry, and even if I was. I didn't feel like I should be ingesting anything that came from her. Nor from anyone else in that house, ever again. I don't know how long it was after that, that I was still there before I got out, or even how I got out. I lost all track of time. After waking up in the hospital, it took me quite a bit more time to figure out that I was not still in the house and that the people who were around and about me. Was there trying to help me rather than to "do me in..." She paused. "In the same manner as did my beloved parents." She whispered this part. "Did my mother hit me over the head with the pot? I'm having a hard time with that one but..." Again, she paused.

"Who else could have done it? It was just us three who were in the house at the time, as far as I could tell. And I... I did see her with the pot though. I thought that she was going to cook. Or something like that. Never would have thought..."

"I don't know if they did anything like force-feed me anything while I was out of it. But I would never consciously eat anything from them again. Or sleep under the same roof with either of them. But Kamal, what did Kamal do? I... I don't understand!" Too much sand around under which to hide her head I suppose. That was where she clammed up though. I wasn't going to get much more out of her, from there. If there's more? I guess that with time, we'll hear it. Along with the rest of that wacky ole story.

In keeping with my promise to her to tell her what I knew, and when I knew it. I then ventured into telling her, in a piecemeal approach. All that I knew and heard from that fateful night up until the current time.

...

The charges

The Dahousts, (all except for the young expectant mother and wife of Kamal.) Like, the cabbie, too, was later charged jointly with criminal acts against their daughter and sister - Libby. The charges ranged from attempted murder, abduction, and detention, to cruel and inhumane treatment. Administering noxious and poisonous substances with intent to cause grievous harm. All the way through to kidnapping. Holding someone against their will, amongst others. With each passing day and with each new report coming in. the charges just keep on piling up on them. They were remanded in custody without bail. Selma though,

Kamal's young wife was not charged in any of this and was sent home. To care for her young child and a soon-to-be-delivered second child. She's going to need all of the help she can get.

...

"According to the intelligence gathered," said the cops. "All of the activities surrounding the case took place in and around the main living quarters of the Dahousts family home. Whatever input Kamal had on any of this was either by way of a telephone call or he would have been present there in person with the rest of the planning committee. On the other hand. Selma was never present in those settings, it would seem. And furthermore, she hardly even seemed to speak a word in English." So there was to be no evidence to suggest to them that she had any input into their devious schemes and plans. Hence, she was sent home.

There are some grave concerns from this point on. For the most relevant parties of interest, as it is. In regard to what shall become of her, Selma, and her young child. Soon to become children with the imminent arrival of the second child. She, being a stranger in a strange new country where she doesn't speak the local language, and now? Suddenly she finds herself faced with the removal of her entire family support structure. It's not going to be easy for her. Will they be able to get her some help? Will Libby be inclined to help her out after all that has happened to her, and against her? Only time will tell.

Chapter Twenty-five: Watching Over Libby.

Selma wasn't the only one who was to have ended up in need of home care. There were some big things happening in my neck of the hood too.

Look, look at him. Norm, my little baby brother, isn't so little anymore. The last time I saw him was five years ago. He was celebrating his twenty-fifth birthday then, look at him now, wow! A very fine young man he has turned out to be after all. Tall, dark, and handsome. He's one shade lighter than me. Hazel eyes. Finely attired to match the fine banking job he has managed to land himself in Toronto. He's easygoing, to a fault.

Norm showed up at my house to spend the Sunday with Libby and me. Although she would not admit it. I saw Mom's fingerprints all over these things. Mom has been doing more than her fair share to help out since Libby moved in with me and I can't thank her enough. So this is Norm's turn to play caregiver. But it would seem as if he was far more interested in caring for himself and helping himself with everything and anything he could get his paws on in the house. Rather than helping and caring for Libby and me, it's all good now. Nothing too good for the good old Norman Whitley.

He made breakfast and a late breakfast it was. More like brunch to me, considering the timing. Scrambled eggs and bacon it was. Easy enough. Libby had cereal. I insisted on preparing Sunday dinner. I had it all planned out from the previous day. Juicy, tender sirloin steak

"

with steamed Brussels sprouts, asparagus, and bitter herbs. Alongside: potatoes (whole potatoes, not mashed.) Carrots and beans, white rice among other things. For those who wanted to have mashed potatoes. I told them, "Go mash it yourself, or be sure to chew each bite well enough to get it as close to mashed potatoes as you can get before swallowing." No one complained, so, I took it that they did enjoy it in the end after all. Libby and Norm did the dishes afterward. I was secretly watching over her the whole time. There was probably no reason for me to be so overly protective of her but then again...

Libby's recovery has been going great. And though I was trying to get her to take things easy and slow. She was not buying that approach at all and said she was not waiting for her recovery to lead her along. She's leading (or more like, dragging.) She was dragging her recovery along instead.

After dinner, we had some good moments of chatting, laughing, and sharing jokes over a game of cards. Sure, it felt good to beat up on Norm once again after all these years. But all good things must come to an end, as they say. So, we bade our farewells and parted. Norm went back to Mom's place for the night. He'll be hitting the road home before the sun is out tomorrow morning. That leaves us with just two. Libby and I in what is a now-familiar setting. I have to make sure she takes her medication and tucks her safely into her bed before I go off to my own bed.

Of late, she has been gradually cutting back on the amount, or on the frequency of those medicinal dosages. I was wary of her doing that because I'd always taken the view that: the physicians know far more than I do, what they are doing. And if they say: "take this," you take it. You don't want to go against the doctor's order just because - at the present moment it may make you feel a bit better doing so. Only to find out later on that what you were doing was contributing to a process that was setting you back, a thousand years, even. Yeah! I know, it's a bit exaggerated. But you get the point I'm making. Right? However, I must hasten to say that. I've come to notice that whenever she does cuts back on the dosage or the frequencies. The difference in terms of her: looking, acting, and feeling better, is undeniable.

This particular evening, however. After my brother had left us to go back to my mom's place. I did notice a somewhat withdrawn crankiness or reservation in her mood. Or something closely akin to that. I couldn't quite put my finger on it, but it was there.

"Do you think I'm pretty?" she asked under her breath. Taken aback, I halted abruptly in my tracks and stared at her.

"What... what?" I stumbled over the words.

"Nothing," she said. Well, it wasn't 'nothing,' it was big. I knew it right away. It was huge." I've been around long enough to know that much: when a woman says nothing is wrong. It's as close as you will probably ever get to everything being wrong. So, I gave her all of my attention. I went and sat right by her side and dug in. "Tell me hon, what's on your mind, what's bothering you?"

"Aren't you even a little bit curious? How come you never..." Stop.

"Never what?" I inquired further, even though I was beginning to sense what the real issue was.

"You never look at me, I mean really look at me."

"Come on Lib. That's not true, you know that is not true."

"Okay, okay, so, maybe I'm stretching it a little bit here, but what I mean is..."

After a long pause,

"I want you to join me for a bath, tonight," she said. I sat there and gazed into her eyes for a good two to three minutes without another word.

"Wait right there," I whispered across her turned-up gaze, as I went into the bathroom and set up a bubble bath. For the next half hour, not a single word was spoken further between us. I set the bath, leaving the tub to fill up to the desired mark. Went and got fresh towels, and lit a fragrant candle in the bathroom. Then after coming back into the room and sitting beside her again, I gazed deep into her eyes, she was shaking. It wasn't the ill effects of the medicine this time. I could tell.

I reached out and took hold of her shoulders and pulled her in towards me as I leaned in to meet her, we kissed, gently, tenderly. I slowly pulled back, to focus on undoing the buttons on her blouse and opening it up. "Won't be needing these in the bathtub you know," I said in low tones, then turned to do the same for me. Undoing the buttons on my shirt. She just sat there with her hands on her lap, head hanging low. Not daring to look at me, yet.

I peel my shirt off and toss it aside. Then did the same for the already opened-up blouse, she shook and shivered some more. I leaned in and hugged her closely, skin to skin. I wanted her to feel the warmth within. I knelt down in front of her and pulled at the slack she was wearing. She eased slightly upwards and backways to allow for it to go. Then, I removed my own pants. She would not look at me, not directly anyway. I knew that she was sneaking a peek whenever the opportunity arose though. I peeled away the bra starting off with the strap on the shoulders, then span it around and unhitched the hooks. Yeah, look. Now we're both equally attired. Both of us sporting only one piece of clothing. It was as close to the Adamic scene in the garden as the two of us had ever been before.

I picked her up and carried her into the bathroom. As I was walking into the bathroom carrying her. She began to sing a sweet little song in my ear: tonight, I celebrate my love for you. And the midnight sun is gonna come shining through... I joined in at the most appropriate point for me: what I want most to do, is to make love to you... tonight. It was magical. (Adapted lyrics, I lay no claim to the same)

She stepped in and slid under the mushy bubbles while still hanging onto my hand. I stepped in with her. She threw both arms around my neck and pulled me in for a hot, wet, lingering kiss. Then we both leaned our backs into the support of the tub and sat there.

"You know." I interrupted the silence. "I've been dreaming of a moment such as this but..."

"But what?"

"I did sort of envision some other things happening before we got to this part."

"Like what?"

"Best if I leave that as it is, enough spoilers already for one night."

We were to spend the rest of the night together, in her room, all night, in her bed. She just wanted to feel my body close to hers she'd said. To hold me, touch me, and squeeze me really tight. She did it, I mean, we did all that, and more? Yes.

The trial should wrap up in a few days, and the verdict is expected to be handed down in court afterward. Libby said she's planning on being there in person to hear it for herself.

Chapter Twenty-Six: So You're Back?

Easter weekend was fast approaching. It has been quite a while since the coming of all of those events. The Dahousts already had a couple of dates with the long arm of the law and were remanded in custody. Libby and I had by then been getting really comfortable with the new arrangements. Like, where she's now living in my house. She's still in recovery mode, but in my house anyway. There really is a god somewhere I believe, and I must have found a little bit of favor with him, (or her). Look at her, she's a far cry from where she was when she first came to me. In terms of her getting better. She also seemed to be getting more and more comfortable with the setting each day.

...

A lot of dates have been popping up around us in recent times. A few pleasant ones but most of them have been of the unpleasant types for Libby and me. A year has come and gone since we went to see the flick at the outdoor cinema complex in Laval. It was one of those dates that had started out really well for us but then. Things were to take a turn for the worse and kept tumbling downhill from then on.

We did try to celebrate this day by focusing mostly on the good parts of that day. We went out to see a movie. Not at the same venue in Laval as before but just a short bus ride away. Down at the cinema complex in Montreal. She did not enjoy it at all. Not because it wasn't a good movie flick. But more so because of the many unpleasant memories it was stirring up for her. At least that's what I'd thought. Although she did not say so at the time. She had been getting the feeling of an airy uneasiness in the place. I was thinking to myself that she was being drawn back to that evening and all of the unpleasant things that were to have happened to her. In her own home and elsewhere since then, and all of it was as a result of her going out to see a movie with her friend. The very same friend with whom she was to be still sitting there in the cinema and watching another not-so-good movie flick. I was there thinking that that was how she was beginning to see it. She had enough of it way before we had gotten to the halfway point of the movie. She didn't want to see any more of it so we skipped the scene and went home.

For the next little while. Her life was going around in circles like a roller coaster. The ride was that bumpy. It was the one-year anniversary of one bad memory after another. Dotted here and there, of course. With a few pleasant ones but still, not enough of those types to compensate sufficiently for the way-too-many bad ones. I was really glad to have learned that I was being featured prominently in most of the pleasant ones and not so much in the bad ones. Amongst the not-so-pleasant memories that were to feature prominently in her mind after that our night out on the town was the one where she was locked up in her own home. God knows how long. Being abandoned and left alone on several occasions. To die maybe? And in the hospital? How happy she was to be to see Manley, (me,) at the hospital, and to have learned that I was there all along. While she was there in the hospital. And that I was actively trying to get her the help that she needed and ultimately, trying to get her out of there. And then, when the time finally came, I was still there, still active, still ready, still very willing and able to take her out of there and into my own home to continue her recovery, if nothing more. This was a special time for both of us, a memorable date. So I decided to take her out and go celebrate it somewhere else. Nothing too elaborate, we agreed. Just a night out on the town.

We were having a fantastic time at the bar. She was laughing away as she used to in the old times, and then. He caught her eye. She swallowed hard against the grit in her mouth. The man was sitting there on the barstool. In the far corner by himself. Sipping Rye whiskey or something like that. He was watching her; he was watching both of us. I didn't notice him, but Libby did. He smiled at me when my gaze followed Libby's and landed on him. He smiled again at Libby who was turning pale and turning around every now and then to look at him. He just keeps on smiling. Showing off a bunch of mal-aligned, rusted old teeth. But rarely (if ever) did the smile touch anywhere near his eyes. Those eyes were cold and scary. Libby was shaking hard from being north of mildly disturbed. I knew it was time to go. So, we hailed a taxi.

"That guy is up to no good," she said as we were en route home. We took a taxi back home just like we did on the way there. We didn't drive because we knew that we would probably both be somewhat intoxicated and incapacitated by the time we were done and ready to get back home. No thanks, though, to the strange-looking loner on the bar stool. We were not as incapacitated as we had thought that we would have been.

"There's something about that guy," said Libby again. "I can't quite put my finger on it but something about him is gnawing at my psyche." We went home and went straight to bed, but not to sleep, yet. Not straight away anyway. We weren't that drunk. No, we weren't drunk at all. As a matter of fact, we didn't stay long enough to get drunk. I had a bottle of bourbon in the cupboard, so I went and fetched it.

"We did plan on getting ourselves stoned tonight," I said, "...and since we never did manage to pull it off at the bar. We might as well just get it done in-house, there's nothing to stop us from doing that, is there?"

"I don't suppose there is."

So I popped it open. Pour a small one for her and one for me. We sat up in bed with our backs rested up against the headrails and supported by pillows as we sipped the liquor. She wasn't into it though. She was obviously still very disturbed. And then, abruptly. She sat up straight and turned to look at me. "That's it!" She said.

"That's What?" I asked. "That's what?"

"The cabbie, that guy looks an awful lot like the cabbie to me."

"What cabbie?" I asked further. Because, in my mind's eye, I could only see the taxi guy who had not too long ago dropped us home, and he bears no resemblance to the guy in the bar, not in the least. But Libby was not talking about that taxi guy. It was another taxi guy that she had in mind, obviously.

"The taxi driver who came to get me on that awful night..." she continued. "The one who they'd locked up along with..."

She didn't bother to finish the statement. She clammed up; she could not finish. Not the statement, and not the drink. She was done for the night. I did my best to reassure her that she was safe here with me and to calm her down, but she refused to be comforted. But then. We went into investigation mode. We needed to find out if there were new developments in the case and on the status of those convicts. Those who were convicted for the many crimes against her. They were all still very much on the inside, as records were to show. There was still some talk of appeals or pending appeals by lawyers, but as for the convicts themselves? They were probably appealing to the tender mercies of their god or various gods daily. But they were to be doing so from behind those prison walls where they were incarcerated. I must admit though. I myself was more than a little bit concerned about the latest developments, but I could not allow my inner feelings to show. I had to be brave and strong for her, for both of us, as a matter of fact. It had become customary by then for me to spend some nights with her. In her room, in her bed. This was obviously one such occasion when that would be well warranted. Together, we bedded down for the night. It was probably due to the effects of the liquor we were drinking earlier. But we were sort of in the mood. Yes, that kind of mood.

So, I whispered many sweet nonsensical things in her ears. Trying to take her mind off the many current concerns, or was it? I told her about the things that I wanted to do. Describing in detail the things I would do to her. Things she would want me to do to her. Things she would beg me to do to her. If and when she'd let me. And then... She let me. So, I... I kissed her there, and then there. And yep, there too, and then... We fused into each other and melted.

...

We were getting ready to go to Toronto for the weekend. This trip was to be more than just a family get-together, you know. My brother had said that he had some big announcements to make, and he wanted the entire family to come down for the weekend to hear it. In fact, the entire family he was referring to is just his mother, his sister, and his brother. That's a lot less hair-raising than when one hears those words - the entire family, isn't it? Saying, the entire family. Makes it sound somewhat like a trailer load of people who would have been involved. More or less, something like what one might hear in some song that an artist or DJ, from somewhere. Whose name would probably be something like Shabba or something like that, would sing about. But saying that, my mother, my brother, and my sister as well as a spouse or two somewhere amongst them. And a young child or two, thrown in here and there. That sounds like something a whole lot more manageable and intimate, doesn't it?

My sister Amy, along with her son Zachary and Mom, went down Thursday night. Libby and I? We were to be going Friday night into Saturday morning. "I'm driving down after work," I told my mom. I needed to see about Libby to make sure she took her medication and tried to get a couple of hours of sleep before we hit the road. I even had to get the car shampooed and vacuumed on the way home from work too. Libby was adamant that she wasn't going to be traveling to Toronto in that dirty car.

"It's not that dirty." I'd said, "And even if we wash it now. It's going to be just as messy by the time we get to Toronto."

"By those kinds of logic," she countered. "We shouldn't wash the dishes, or the clothes, or even clean the house. Because they all are going to get messed up again too, won't they?"

Couldn't argue with that. So off to the carwash I had to go. All in all, we should be pulling out of Montreal at some time around ten or ten-thirty. We're in no hurry to get there, we'll just take it nice and easy. Should get there around five thirty or six on Saturday morning. Perfect for me to get into the day's activities, perfect for both of us, I had said.

Norm has been moving up the ladder of success like a monkey up a banana pole. He has been moving up in the world by leaps and bounds in recent times. Bought himself a brand-new house out there in Brampton, Ontario. And although young, Mr. Whitley has been very tight-lipped about the price tag. I've done my research and I can comfortably guess it to be at least somewhere in the $2.5 million to $3 million price bracket. Could easily be more too, not less. He had just moved in and wanted to christen the house. Or as he called it: "breaking in" the house. Along with his closest friends and family around him, great. But that wasn't all that Mr. Whitley had up his sleeve. Norm was planning on getting hitched and wanted to introduce his wife-to-be to his next of kin. Audrey is her name. Audrey Snowden. A beautiful blonde-haired blue-eyed girl who is into banking just like him. Both are quickly climbing up the ladder into middle management positions in the world of banking and money management. Wish them well. Will you?

This was to be the first time that Libby was meeting my sister Amy. As well as her son - Zach.

"What a sweet little boy," she'd said. "How come you never told me about him?"

"I never did, like, tell anyone about my folks, unless they asked, and you never asked."

"How could I ask if I didn't know?"

"That's the conundrum, the irony of things right there, you see. People are supposed to seek in order to find, they say. But one doesn't usually go about seeking just for the sake of seeking and, or, of finding. Usually, one tends to know exactly what they are seeking out. One will seek out what one already knows or knows about. Do you want to hear some more irony here though? I do believe that Norm is fixing to get himself hitched. I myself was hitched once before, and neither of us has got any children, yet. Or at least, not that I know of, but Amy, who has never been married, is the one who has managed to make uncles out of us both. She said that she's not in any hurry to complicate her life. She's doing quite well as it is.

I've got a strange feeling that I have something to do with her fear of commitment though. She never took the breakup of my marriage with Aylene very well. Come to think of it, she hasn't been able to have had very much of a good experience with any of the men in her life either, it would seem. Dad wasn't a good role model in that arena and me...? Pause.

Amy is doing very well for herself. She's got a good job working with Revenue Canada. And she's doing a great job raising her son all by herself, seemingly. Amy and Mom traveled down to Toronto together. "No need for two cars," she had said, "not when one will suffice."

I watched as Mom dabbed at a tear or two at several intervals as the evening progressed. I think they were tears of joy and triumph. Oh! How she must have pitied those two losers who'd thought that they could have done better without her. She's got an awful lot to be thankful for. In spite of everything, in spite of me, even. She hasn't done too badly after all. For a young woman to have picked herself up. Left her job, her native country, and all of the people whom she knew and loved, and then took her two young children and migrated to a foreign country. With little more than the clothes on her back, and not even having anyone with whom she'd have prior acquaintances living in that foreign country. On whom she could rely for support or just to show her the ropes and to get the ship anchored properly there. That was a very risky thing to do. But she did it, and just look at her and her children today. Remarkable I'd say, remarkable indeed.

Norm and Audrey were not just casually seeing each other as it turned out. They're in fact engaged. She's sporting a shiny glistening piece of rock. Wow, how lovely is that? We almost felt a bit out of place amongst the guests. The darker shades of our faces stood out like a sore thumb amongst them but that was the hang-ups we felt. It was all on our account, the discomfort too, the cuteness. We were never made to feel like we did not belong there. Not by Norm, not by Audrey, and not by any of the many guests present there. But, as for us...?

Old boy Norm seemed to have a knack for picking his friends and associates very well indeed. The stakes have been raised, expectations level bumped up a notch or two on in-house measuring instruments. No words were ever spoken in this regard, but the actions were screaming, and it all seemed to be saying-time to step up to the plate, mister man. As in, Manley.

My business is doing okay. Been taking some hits since Libby came home but still. I can't complain, she's, my girl. And she's well worth it in my eyes. My heart and in my soul. I love this woman loads and I'm just going to have to do right by her if nothing else I ever get to do in this messed-up world.

Her recovery has been phenomenal. I couldn't have been happier for her, for us. I can clearly see a day on the horizon. And it's fast approaching. A day when we can move forward to the next level in our relationship. All of the signals on those fronts have been looking good for all concerned.

I'd promised Libby that I was going to marry her soon, "as soon as possible," I had said. Or as soon as she became well enough. That was quite a while ago and by the looks of things. She's well enough as it now is. As a matter of fact, I think she's better than "well and good enough." She's fully recovered, I'd say.

I have surely got some big decisions to make over the next little while. The money flow has dried up somewhat, but I have the work and lots of it. So, it will be just a matter of time before the money will be coming in again, I'd consoled myself.

...

"When last have you heard from Dad?" Amy asked.

She kept her head straight in the taillights ahead of her. Mom did not respond. After a quick glance at her mother sitting there to the right of her, she rephrased the question and asked again.

"Have you heard from Dad recently?"

"What are you talking about-Amy?"

"Cal. Calvin Woodhardt, our father! That's what, that's who. Have you heard from him in recent times?"

"No Amy, why? Why are you asking?" She shot back with more than a hint of annoyance in her voice.

"Why are you asking about him now, after all these years?"

"Nothing, it's just that..."

"Just that what?"

"Nothing Mom, never mind, let's just forget about it."

"No, no, what's going on? Why did you ask?"

"He's been calling me of late - Mom, I don't know how he did manage to track me down, but he just called me up out of the blue a while back and has been calling ever since."

"How long has this been going on? I mean, really? How long has it been since? Since. Since he crawled back into your life trying to beguile you and the rest of us? When did all this start?"

"It's been a while back, he just called me up out of the blue and said he was trying to get in touch with us, with you, even. He wanted to get in touch with you and his children for quite some time. Someone must have given him my number. I never get to find out who such a 'someone' might have been but, he has been calling me ever since. I suppose we owe all of this to the information age in which we now live. At first, he'd said that he just wanted to find out how we were doing. And that he was sorry for not being there for us when we were young, but he said that he would like to make it up to us. I was kind of happy to hear from him and to have him showing some interest in me, in us. But now..."

"Now what?" Ask Mom as she momentarily steps back from under the fountain of not-so-pleasant memories where she'd bolted since Amy opened up the conversation.

"Now what?"

"Now he's asking for money."

"I knew it, I just knew it."

"He said his health is deteriorating, and the medical expenses are draining him. And he wants us to help him out."

"Well, well," said Mom, while she was turning her head around to look at her grandson sleeping there in the backseat of the car. "You had better not be even thinking of doing any such thing. There! Right there is where your responsibilities lie, with him." She said while pointing at Zach. "That man never gives a shit what happened to you, or to any of us when he could have. He was much more interested in running around like a puppy dog chasing after every other skirt tail that might just happen to pass by. Let him go to them now for the help he needs."

"But ma..."

"But Ma nothing, you just listen to me and stay the hell away from him and his problems. They're not yours, nor mine. So, don't you go about picking up those bundles that aren't yours. Your loyalty is to-wards your young son. Not to a man whom you hardly even know who just happened to show up or call out of the blue to say, 'I'm your daddy and I need your help.' Where was he when you needed a daddy? Where was he when you needed his help? I'll tell you, running around like a blooming puppy dog. Chasing after every woman and her skirt tail. Leave that no-good son-of-a-bitch to his own devices, and to his cheating, lying web of deceit that he weaves with his own two hands. It's not yours to fix, none of it is, nor is it mine. It doesn't belong to any of us, so you leave him and his problems well the hell alone and place your focus on yourself and on your young child, where it rightfully belongs."

"I'm sorry mom, I never knew that he'd hurt you that badly."

"This is not about me, so just leave me out of it - please."

"But it is about you - Mom, it's about all of us."

"I don't want you to go through this life being a weakling - Amy. Someone that everybody can just come and use and abuse and laugh at. You must be strong. Strong enough to be able to say no to people whose every thought and motivation in life is to use and abuse you and then leave you to suffer. You've suffered enough at the hands of Calvin Woodhardt already as it is. We all have. Though you may not be able to remember or place things in their proper perspective now since you were so young when we had to up and leave. But trust me on this one, stay away from that man."

"Does Manley know about any of this?" She asked after an extended pause.

"No, I don't think so, I really don't know for sure. Since I haven't spoken to him on this, but he probably has. He might have called him up by now."

"What makes you think that? Did you give him Manley's number?"

"Matter of fact, I did. He asked - Mom, he outright asked for it. At the time, I never did see it as being a problem. I thought that he would have loved to hear from his father too, just like I was..."

"That boy," she muttered under her breath. "He's becoming just a little bit too much like his deadbeat daddy for my liking," she said, then she sighed, and groaned agonizingly.

"Something has got to give," I heard someone say. Who was it that had said so? Can't quite remember. But...

Chapter Twenty-seven: The Trial, and More Trials.

In their defense. The Dahousts claimed that it was Libby who had tried to kill herself. By swallowing sleeping pills, and the noxious windshield washer fluid. In an attempt at getting out of the arranged marriage to someone whom she didn't know. Like she was heard to have said to some people. Like she had said that she would do if they, her parents, ever were to try to marry her off like they did her brother.

"So, you're here telling this Court," Her lawyer counteracted, "that your daughter and sister: Libby Dahoust. Who was on the fast track to a promising career in the medical field, and who was madly in love with someone whom you, (coincidentally,) did not approve of? Someone who just happened to show up at your door on the very evening when your daughter was last seen alive and well. Until she was rescued by law enforcement officers bound and nearly dead in her house, her own home, or what should have been so, like, 'her home.' Your daughter, who was considering moving out of your house to go out and fend for herself. She suddenly gets the bright idea that it's better to go bind and lock herself in the basement. Swallow a handful of sleeping pills. Along with a whole lot of windshield washer fluid and whatever else she could find just hanging around the room that would fast-track the process. And all this, while her hands were tied behind her back?" They insisted, though, that although it may not have followed those orders and sequences. Their version of events were the facts as they had occurred. There are several witnesses who can testify to the fact that

that's what she had said that she would do if they should try to marry her off as they had done to Kamal.

"Do you love your daughter Mr. Dahoust? I repeat the question. Do you love, or even like, do you 'like' your daughter?"

"I love all my children."

"I see, and, armed with those facts," he continued, "those facts that you've just told this Court. You then went and did the very thing that you said she had told you that she didn't want you to do to her, and for her. And had even given you ample warnings. According to your own words, if you ever try to do it, she would in return do something terrible to herself. Armed with all of that knowledge, you then went on to do the exact same thing, that she said would solicit those responses on her part. You did that to your child, to your own daughter whom you told us that you love so very much. Then went about taking steps to finish off the job and cover your tracks..."

"Objection..." An objection was quickly mounted by the defense. Upon objection from the defense lawyer. He quickly ventured out to withdraw those comments.

...

The verdict. Found guilty of all charges. This was the verdict for all four of the accused. Libby and I were there on the day the verdict was being read in court. She was out of the intensive care unit by then and was staying at my place most of the time. She wanted to see the proceedings live and in person. It did take some persuading on a number of different fronts, but the care team at the hospital did eventually agree to send her with me to court on the day of the verdict.

The convicts were being escorted out of the courthouse in handcuffs by security guards. Libby and I were standing near the exit when he saw us. Mr. Dahoust saw me standing there with his daughter. The same daughter whom he, his wife, best friend, and his son were arrested and charged, and has now been found guilty of her attempted murder. He saw us standing there, together and halted his steps in the doorway.

"Son of a bitch," he said, staring at me standing there with his daughter who could have, and probably should have died, for all he cared.

Thanks to none other than him, her very own sweet loving father, and them, her mother, and her ever-loving brother. His piercing eyes, with such scorn, venom, and guile, just like a sword it was cutting at me.

"...No sir," I replied in my - by then fast-becoming the usual manner. "No sir, I said, you ain't know nothing about me, nor my mother. Or anyone else on my family tree for that matter. So don't you go comparing me to whatever it is that your idea of a family is. Or ought to be."

The sentencing, if there was any surprise in anybody's mind. It would have been in the length of the sentences. The amount of time each will have to serve. Especially for the younger Dahoust male. He could be out in less than five years. Thirty-five years without any chance of parole for ten years, for the parents and their friend, the taxi driver. Twenty years for Kamal, with his first chance at parole after serving four. Not nearly enough in the minds of most people, as the reports and comments in the papers and elsewhere would suggest. But that's where things are for the time being.

Lawyers for both the senior Dahousts as well as Kamal had all been giving notices of appeal. At least as was to be heard coming in rhetoric at this point.

Chapter Twenty-eight: Down But Not Out.

We were descending the steps at the courthouse when I lost my footing and fell. My well-choreographed script, played out just as I had planned. I rolled down the last three steps to the pavement below. Libby was screaming as she hobbled down in the best way she could and stood over me looking into my sneaky eyes. And me, grinning all over my face while lying there. She offered me a hand up. I took it, not so much for the support role she had intended but more for what I was about to do next. I got "up" to my knees from the position where I was lying there on my back. While still holding onto her right hand with my left hand. I flipped open the tiny black box in my right hand. "Libby sweetheart," I said. "Will you marry me?"

With her left hand covering her mouth, and her body convulsing. Pulsating in a cross mix of her trying to suppress the laughter and the tears. She did manage to squeeze out a couple: "Yes, yes, y..."

Before I stopped her in her tracks with a hot lingering kiss. To a chorus of oohs, aahs, and clapping cheers.

We eventually left the courthouse and headed home. We were both going back to my place Downtown. We drove by the store in Cote des Neige. She just wanted to see the place. She doesn't seem to have the same strong feeling of resentment about the shop as she does the house. Said she was going to call Selma, Kamal's wife, and try to talk to her about it to see if she has any ideas that could get the place up and running again. "I don't want to have anything to do with it," she said. But Selma is a stranger in a strange new country. Someone who suddenly found herself alone with a young family to care for all on her own. She's going to need all the help that she can get." Libby had said that she was willing to reach out to her brother's wife and help in any way that she could.

"She's a good girl," she said. She didn't deserve any of this."

Libby was released and placed into my care and protection after the hospital had managed to assure themselves that it was, in fact, in the best interest of the patient. Or maybe it was because they were left with no other option. After Libby's insistence that she was not going back to spend another night in that house, ever again.

She's now staying in my spare room. Recovering quite nicely indeed. Everyone concerned has been in agreement that, so far, she's doing quite well. And she really likes her new friend, Doctor Peppers. The new puppy I'd bought her as a welcome home present. It is more than just a welcome home present. It's in fact, a lot more than a pet for her at this point. The dog is now a helper, aiding her along in the recovery effort during the long walk back to her optimal health.

Doctor Peppers is as cranky as I am this evening. So, as you all already know, it's time to go walking. After a long and hectic day at the courthouse. Libby has already had more than enough activities today to compensate for her daily exercises. So, it's now my turn to go and walk the Doctor. Dr. Peppers that is.

As we turned the corner, the puppy and me. I noticed the four women standing there on the pavement near the park benches smoking and chatting away. And they were not the least bit discreet, either. I knew right away what the topic of their discussion was. The news was spreading like wildfire.

"He proposed to her on the steps of the courthouse. During the trial of her parents." One of those blabbermouths was heard to have said.

"So did she accept?" Another wanted to know. "Did he go down on one knee?"

And then. Yet another one of them said. "If a guy is going to propose to me, he had better be doing it right, or else, no dice."

Then yet another thought that she knows the best time and ways of doing it. "On New Year's Eve or, New Year's Day in proper, and sealed with a kiss." The discussion continued as they started to fade out of my earshot.

I couldn't help but wonder how many of those know-it-alls have done it and are still basking in the afterglow. The after-effects of the whole process, you know, hmm.

Meanwhile, Dr. Peppers hoisted a leg up on the signpost and shot off a few squirts of pee. Couldn't have been more perfect for me, the timing. I wanted to hear more from these toddle-tales. So, I even allowed him to sniff around as much as he wanted to do afterward. Before moving on, slowly, very slowly indeed. Until I was too far out of earshot range to hear anything more from them. It didn't really matter to me though, what they were thinking, saying, or even feeling on the subject. I guess it was just one of those strange phenomena where you hear or see something familiar and by reflection, you just have to react. Sort of like. You hear your name or someone speaking in a familiar language or dialect. In a crowded place among people who all speak languages other than your own. It's like music to your ears, that familiar language or dialect will grab you every time. And cause you to stop, turn around, and dig in closer for more. That was all that was meant to be for me. I just went along my merry way, walking the doctor, Doctor Peppers.

We went right along singing away:

One man went to mow, woof, woof,

Went to mow the meadow, woof, woof,

One man and his dog, woof, woof,

Went to mow the meadow, Woof, woof. (Adapted, I lay no claim to this)

Am I just imagining things here or is there really a bit more pep in both our steps today? Both Doctor Pepper and me?

The end.

For feedback, email us at contact: elkthepoet@gmail.com. The author really wants to hear from you, his readers.

Extras

Note from the author. Just a note of thank you for choosing to read my book and for sticking with the story thus far. You must have liked it a lot. At this point, I want to ask you, my reader, to take a minute or two to post a review of the book on the Sales pages at Amazon and any other such sales pages. This small gesture is so very much appreciated. And don't keep it to yourself, be sure to share this. Thank you.

More notes: some lines and quotes in this book may be recognized as familiar lines from some well-known (or not-too-well-known) songs. We lay no claim to the ownership of these materials and only use them on the assumption of a "fair-use," basis. And out of pure love and admiration for the pieces and in some cases, the authors. Should the rights owners have issues with our usage of any of these pieces, just let us know and we will make the necessary efforts to rectify the situation, or remove the offending pieces, as may be possible now-a-day. Thank you very much. Special thanks to these people who have helped in various ways in bringing about this book. Thanks to my immediate as well as the extended family: To Leonie and Charles who had to put up with me not being quite there at times, even when I might have been there in the body. In the end, your support was unwavering and unmistakable. Thank you. To my church family who supported me by allowing me the time, space and also physically, by spending your hard-earned cash to purchase the books or by telling others about them. Thank you ever so much.

So why do I write? You'd asked. The answer is: I'm a guy of many words, but whose tongue is slow and heavy, and my words tend to come out awkward and clumsy, so I write, because I always have something to say, I think. Which always tends to get me into trouble anyway. The extra bonus though, in writing, is that a pencil usually comes with an eraser.

E Lloyd Kelly is the writingelk

E Lloyd Kelly is an author, poet, and blogger. Born in Jamaica, West Indies, to Raglan and Alma Kelly. Now resides in Montreal Quebec where (when not writing,) he drives a shuttle bus between campuses at McGill University.

Other works by E Lloyd Kelly, include;

Backsliding

The sword, the word, and books of rules (free gift on the website.)

The Shirt Depot

Black blood,

76: Clancy's journey,

Some Shitty Vacation,

Waters of Silver Springs and

Spaces, my space, your space and the public space:

Find these on the Author's page at Amazon.com/author/elloydkelly, http://www.amazon.com/-/e/B01G7NYWL6

#yardcoresextalk of a teenage boy and the encounters he was to have had with women while on his journey into manhood. How his life was shaped, and the folks whose hands helped in shaping him. Keep the mind sharp, start by reading something, anything, but we'd sure like it if you read our books on: amazon.com/author/elloydkelly. This is a copyright-protected material. All rights reserved.

Printed in the USA
CPSIA information can be obtained
at www.ICGtesting.com
LVHW021213101223
765728LV00077BA/1865